Liberty Frye
∞ and the ∞
Emperor's Tomb

OTHER BOOKS BY J.L. MCCREEDY:

Liberty Frye and the Witches of Hessen (Book One)

Liberty Frye and the Sails of Fate (Book Two)

The Orphan of Torundi

BOOK THREE

Liberty Frye
∞ and the ∞
Emperor's Tomb

J.L. McCreedy

PENELOPE PIPP PUBLISHING

Published by Penelope Pipp Publishing

www.penelopepipp.com

ISBN: 978-0-9882369-6-7
Library of Congress Control Number: 2018912961

To Lizzy, adventurer and question-asker extraordinaire.

And to Sam, my favorite idea-bouncer, world-wanderer and muse-maker ... among other things.
Thanks for all the magic you bring.

CONTENTS

Contents

CONTENTS

WARNING

But why bother? I will see you at journey's end.

1

İNTO ᴛʜᴇ ɴɪɢʜᴛ

The farmer stared at the ground where three salted fish lay. Then he scowled at a girl who ran like lightning across the field, stuffing duck eggs into her pocket.

"You rascal!" he shrieked after her. "Bring those eggs back this instant!"

"But I just paid for them with the salted mullet!" the girl replied in stilted Chinese. She laughed, now taking a muddy path winding up the hill, not caring that her sandals sank through the slick surface.

The farmer shook his head as he glanced back down at the fish, though he couldn't help chuckling. He was glad his wide hat hid most of his face. He forced his expression into a frown and called after her, "Next time, ask permission first, Ine!"

He tried to keep his tone stern. "It is poor manners to assume a fair trade without both parties agreeing beforehand!"

This was met with another peal of laughter, and then the girl's blonde hair flicked in the sunlight before disappearing from view.

The farmer muttered something to himself about having a talk with Ine's parents. That girl was too often left to her own devices; what kind of young lady was allowed to run free and mad through the village, effecting trades of fish and eggs, no less? And at such a tender age! He shuddered to think what she'd be like in a few more years.

"Too much spirit in her blood," he muttered through his teeth. And with that, the farmer plucked the salted mullet from the ground and stomped toward his cottage.

The girl called Ine ran until she reached the top of a grassy knoll—the same place she came almost every day—then flopped to the ground, still panting. She was careful not to smash the duck eggs. When she'd caught her breath, she rolled to a sitting position, crossed her legs and reached into her pocket once more. This time, she produced a collapsible brass spyglass. It was her prized possession.

Ine pulled at the ends so the spyglass extended to its full length, then lifted it to her right eye. She panned the harbor below, her pale eyes matching the greyish-blue of the sunlit water, searching as she always did for her father's boat.

Although there were at least five boats in the harbor that afternoon, there was one trait that set her father's boat apart from the local fishermen's: the bright yellow and blue of their German family crest. Ine was especially proud of that crest. With the help of her mother, she had painted it on the side of the hull six months ago, along with their surname, "Herrmann," scrolled just beneath.

Ine continued peering through the spyglass at the boats dotting the harbor. She swooped her sight left to right, then right to left, knowing all along that her father wasn't expected back from his mission trip for several days. She looked anyway.

Suddenly, Ine froze mid-swoop. *What have we here?*

In the two years since her family had moved to this village on the east coast of China, only once had she spotted a boat so large. That time, it turned out to be a merchant vessel that had somehow lost its coordinates. So what was the reason for *this* ship? No one ever came here except local fishermen and the occasional visiting government official. Of course, now and then there was the random missionary who had heard of her family's work, but never had any of these arrived in such a magnificent ship.

Ine's heart thrummed with excitement.

She squinted through her spyglass, watching as the ship drew closer, and it almost felt as if her anticipation was the force that pulled it toward the harbor. She could make out the scroll of white letters along the side of the hull now, and strange glints aboard the deck, metal things flashing in the sunlight. How very curious ….

Gently, so gently, Ine collapsed the spyglass. She slipped it into her pocket and rose to her feet. And then she darted down the hill toward the sun-specked harbor.

✻

By the time she reached the inlet where most fishing boats docked, the blue skies had bowed their colors to dusk. Shadows flicked over the wooden walkway as water lapped the sides of boats held to the shore with rope. Ine scurried over the walkway, flinging the mantle of her cape over her head to blend in. The last thing she wanted was for one of her mother's pupils to spot her creeping along the harbor instead of returning home for supper like she knew she should.

Besides, she wasn't hungry. She had something much more important to think about than supper; namely, why on earth was a ship called *Liberté* docked inside this tiny fishing harbor?

From the name alone, she knew it must be French. Thanks to her mother's extensive language skills, Ine was raised speaking German and English, but knew enough French and Italian to get by. She was even making decent progress on the local Chinese dialect.

Back to the *Liberté*, though, for Ine was not to be distracted:

Why was it here? What was it after? How long would it stay?

Ine crept between the ropes, passing fishermen who glanced curiously at the foreign ship silhouetted in the distance. She heard whispers between them: an envoy had already been assigned, one of them declared, and no doubt the entire village would know the ship's business by the time the sun poked over the horizon. Let the merchants and those with too much time on their hands fret and scheme over the ship's arrival, they all agreed; as for them, their bones ached and their muscle throbbed. It was time for dinner, for rest, for the comforts of home.

Ine waited as the fishermen bid one another good evening, their work-weary calls mixing with the sound of lapping water.

And then the inlet was quiet, as if even the boats and the wind and fish and birds and all matter of life we cannot see had tucked in for the night, and the rhythmic slosh of the tide was like their snores of slumber.

But all that was about to change.

Ine stopped at a small boat in the shallow harbor and was just about to unhook the rope anchoring it to shore when, suddenly, she darted behind the boat instead.

"Mensch Meier!" she whispered, too shocked to worry about the frigid water or her soaking clothes, because two boats down from where she crouched was a most peculiar sight:

An old woman had appeared on the shore out of nowhere, carrying a large bundle strapped to her back. The woman was wrapped in a shawl that covered her head and most of her face, making her appearance difficult to work out, though strands of white hair escaped from her shawl, and her stooped posture betrayed her age. Her sudden presence alone was a bit unnerving, but what really took Ine's breath away was what the old woman was watching:

In the foggy distance, a small, wooden boat rocked in the

water, slowly making its way to shore. Something thin and pale stood at the front of the boat, but Ine couldn't quite make it out just yet. Fog tickled the water's surface, stretching and growing its wispy fingers, enshrouding the little boat in mist.

Ine squinted, now making out the figure standing in the center of the approaching boat, and she could see the figure was covered from head to toe in some sort of thin silk. This was unusual, to be sure, but the most uncanny part was that this draped figure had eyes that actually glowed *through* the cloth like two, small lanterns! And as the fog curled and grasped at the air, the figure with those magical, glowing eyes looked like a ghost floating through a sea of vapor.

Ine didn't even realize she was holding her breath as she stared at the boat and the glowing-eyed ghost. Only then did she notice that two other people were on the boat as well. And then a voice broke through the silence:

"I *told* you that disguise wouldn't work!"

Ine floundered in the water in an attempt to get a better look, shocked to hear someone speaking English. She continued to squint through the fog to see a girl with long, brown hair in a tight ponytail glaring at the ghost-thing with magical eyes. The other person on the boat was also a girl, Ine could now determine, but the second girl remained seated at the back, where she was rowing.

"Look what you've done!" the ponytailed girl exclaimed. She appeared to be older than Ine, maybe eleven or twelve. "You've totally blown our cover! There is a woman standing on shore, staring straight at us!"

"How-else-do-you-suggest-that-I-accompany-you-for-translating?" the thing with glowing eyes responded, and even in her puzzled state, Ine couldn't help but notice how oddly the figure spoke.

But just then, the boat hit the shore, not ten feet away from the old woman with the large bundle. The old woman stepped toward the boat and, with shaking arms, lowered the bundle from her back.

"I thought … I might bring this to you," the woman said in the local Chinese dialect, but her voice was pinched into a wheeze, as though she were terribly nervous but forcing herself to speak anyway, and beyond that, she sounded strangely halting, as if the woman struggled to find the right words … or perhaps had forgotten them altogether. "They are … the local garments you currently … seek. No need to … attempt … bartering in the village; you would only cause a stir. Take these and … return to your ship …."

As the old woman spoke, Ine could hear the thing with glowing eyes translating everything into English, presumably for the benefit of the two girls. Even in the increasing darkness, Ine could see the blood drain from their faces.

"How did she know to expect us?" gasped the second girl, rising from her seat on the boat bench. "And how did she know we were looking for clothes? I mean, that's impossible!"

From behind the little fishing boat where she stooped, Ine nodded in agreement without realizing, her eyes as wide as mooncakes. A sense of foreboding crept through her then, like the fog over the harbor. Thoughts of her mother rushed through her mind, and of the cozy fire waiting at home; of their dumpling soup they were sure to have; of the duck eggs in her pocket she intended to surprise her nanny with.

Ine suddenly wanted to go home; she didn't want to crouch in this cold water anymore. She didn't want to witness any more of this unnatural encounter. She wanted to go. No, she *needed* to go; she knew she should, before it was too late ....

As if being pulled from above by an invisible string, Ine rose from behind the fishing boat. For a split second, the old woman, the ghost-person and the two girls all turned to regard her in surprise. Ine gaped back at them all, her entire body shaking as she stood to her full height, her cape dripping with water. And then she leapt toward the wooden walkway.

The ghost-person, though obviously distracted, was still repeating the girl's previous question to the old woman in the local dialect. There was a pause as the old woman watched Ine sprint away.

"*Impossible* you say," the old woman finally rattled in reply, only now, to everyone's surprise, she suddenly spoke in English, and the stilting manner of her speech was gone. She shifted so she directly faced the three figures in the rowboat, her eyes gleaming like two opals, even in the dark. "Isn't the impossible why you are here, Liberty Frye?"

2

THE DARK TOWER

The passage of time is a funny thing. No one shares a single moment in exactly the same way—or at least, that's what Libby had decided.

For example, their sea voyage from the South Pacific to China had, to her, felt like an eternity. She'd long since memorized every spell in the spell book that Sabine, the witch in the woods she'd met while in Germany, had given her, and since there was little else to read on their ship besides a few science journals and Ginny's stash of instruction manuals, Libby was left to worry over other things.

Like her mother.

Despite the fact she and Ginny agreed Libby's separation from her mom was for the best, how would that play out if they were successful in their quest? What would happen when—and if—she finally reunited with her parents? Would her mom suffer again from Libby's connection with Zelna?

Even though Libby had watched her evil great aunt perish in the explosion almost a year ago, it was clear that Zelna's powers had somehow attached themselves to Libby, and that Libby's mom had been sacrificing her own health to fight those same powers off. But then, when the crew of the *Liberté* had accidentally time-traveled on Libby's eleventh birthday—leaving Mr. and Mrs. Frye behind at the Biloxi marina—, it seemed that Libby had somehow taken on the full force of Zelna's powers without her mother's intervention.

Granted, the reality of having been transported to another century was definitely less than ideal for all parties involved, but the realization that this separation was also protecting her mom had been an unexpected perk. And now, Libby wondered if she could continue protecting her mother if she found her way back home. How could she be sure?

She couldn't, that's how. And the knowledge of *that* kept her tossing and turning at night, struggling to find an answer. It didn't help that Ginny was convinced this sleeplessness was less about Mrs. Frye and more about missing Kai, the boy Libby had become friends with in the South Pacific. It was so annoying, but what could Libby say? It was true she'd secretly hoped he might change his mind and join them on their voyage to China, even though she knew his choice to stay behind had been the right one. Of course it was. He belonged to a different world, to a different century. Even so, it was depressing to know that one of the few people she'd ever felt close to was gone from her life forever ....

That's what two months on a ship does to a person: it makes you dwell on all the thoughts and worries you'd rather not consider, and there is nothing you can do about any of it except wait.

And Libby hated waiting.

As for Uncle Frank and Sal, waiting didn't seem to bother them so much. If it weren't for the fact that they were locked in another century and half a world away from Peter and Gretchen Frye, Libby suspected her great uncle and his old war buddy might think this voyage was the adventure of a lifetime ... and one that was flying by far too quickly for their tastes.

"Life's like a roll of toilet paper, kid," Sal often opined. "The closer you get to the end, the faster it goes."

Libby didn't know how to feel about *anyone's* life being compared to toilet paper, but she saw Sal's point. Time for her definitely moved slower than it did for Sal or Uncle Frank. She thought about that a lot, but when she tried to ask Ginny what her thoughts were on the matter, Ginny would just shrug and turn her attention back to the latest *Liberté* Inspection Checklist she'd developed.

As for Buttercup, Libby wondered if the concept of time was even something that registered with him. Did pet geese remember thoughts or experiences in terms of past or present? Did they ever feel young or old or somewhere in between? And did Buttercup even miss Libby's mom and dad?

These questions and others rattled around Libby's brain,

and she wondered if, when they finally found this Wizard Sheng they sought, would he be able to answer any of them? Surely he would. You don't live to be thousands of years old without learning a thing or two. And that's what Libby was banking on: that very soon now, they would find the Wizard on the mountaintop near Qingdao where they had anchored, and then everything about their predicament would change ….

But at this particular moment in time, Libby wasn't thinking about wizards or Buttercup or even of her mother, because the only thing Libby was thinking was:

STOP!

Pain ripped through her sides as she ran. Alleyways snaked between cottages where merry fires glowed, but the cold mist pressed against her like a wet washcloth, pushing into her lungs. She felt dizzy. She could barely breathe anymore, but she didn't slow down. Her boots splashed on the wet, packed earth, her pants now soggy up to her knees. She ran on, panting as she followed the flick of blonde hair that disappeared like smoke around bend after bend.

As she ran, it felt as if she were watching herself from somewhere far away. *What was she doing? Why was she chasing this little girl?*

Libby didn't know why. She knew only this:

As soon as she'd hit the shores of Qingdao with Ginny and Esmerelda, something very strange had happened. For starters, that old woman had inexplicably showed up with their bundle of clothes—a bizarre enough thing in and of itself, but it got downright creepy when the woman called Libby by her name—

and then the next thing Libby remembered was the girl darting over the wooden walkway, away from the inlet and toward the village. In fact, Libby had already jumped out of the rowboat and was chasing after the little girl before she even realized what she was doing, leaving a shouting Ginny and an indignant robot behind.

And now, here she was, sprinting through a tiny fishing village on the east coast of nineteenth-century China in the middle of the night, all for no apparent reason other than the fact she felt certain she had to speak to a scared little girl. Had she totally lost it? It wasn't out of the question. Being stuck on a ship with a couple of cranky old men and a best friend obsessed with safety protocols can really mess with a girl's head ….

Libby turned another corner, now wheezing up a pathway that curled toward a hilltop. And then, miraculously, the little girl slowed down enough for Libby to reach her. She lunged for the girl's wrist, and it wasn't until she had a firm grasp that she glimpsed around and realized they'd stopped beside some sort of tower.

"Let me go!"

"Please!" Libby panted, still clutching the girl's wrist, but something very peculiar happened as soon as she said that. Or perhaps it was as soon as she'd grabbed the girl's wrist, she wasn't sure, but it suddenly seemed as if the girl moved forward several feet—almost like a fast-forward motion—then instantly moved back to her current spot by the tower. And had Libby moved, too? Had they both just repeated their steps from moments before?

"I'm sorry," she blurted. "I don't mean to scare you, but I need to know who you are. It's very important! I-I don't know why, but I—*OW!*"

Libby released her grasp, her hand flying protectively to her chest as the girl turned and ran away, now disappearing into the shadows. And when Libby looked from where the girl had just vanished to her hand, she discovered two red semi-circles with tiny teeth marks blazing on her skin.

It was quite a shock; it had all happened so fast. But there was something about being bitten by a total stranger that brought Libby back to her senses. She looked around, for the first time realizing she had absolutely no idea where she was or how to get back to the harbor.

"What have I done?" she murmured (which, in truth, was a question directed solely at herself), but just then, a creaky, groaning sound came from somewhere above. Libby turned, quite surprised to discover a gnarled chestnut tree not three feet from her path bending down to an almost right angle, as if bowing to her presence.

"Are you … are you able to communicate with me?" she whispered, and though she was alone in a foreign place where no one would have understood her anyway, she felt ridiculous. After all, it was one thing to speak to a tree in the middle of the woods in Germany, and another thing altogether to have a chat with a tree in town.

The tree wiggled the tips of its bare limbs.

Libby gulped in the misty air, her eyes locked on the gnarled tree.

"You're probably …," she finally managed, "uh, waiting for me to ask a question, right?"

The tree wiggled its limbs once more, but it also began twisting more urgently, seemingly pointing in the direction of the tower. This confused Libby at first, but seconds later, she heard voices coming from the path below.

"You're … telling me to hide in the tower? So no one sees me?"

The tree bobbed its branches up and down. Libby glanced uneasily from the tower back to the path where the voices grew closer, and while she suspected her new tree-friend might have a better grasp on what the local attitude was towards time-traveling foreigners who chase children through fishing villages, she did know with absolute certainty that Uncle Frank had made her promise not to draw attention to herself ….

"Okay, um, so … thank you," she murmured, and then she dashed to the tower door, grabbing the thick, circular ring that hung from a brass plate. She pushed her weight against the door, but it didn't budge.

The voices grew closer.

Impatiently, Libby slammed her shoulder once more against the door, all the while silently chiding herself. What had she been thinking? Had she learned nothing at all about time travel? The first rule of thumb was: Avoid interacting with *anyone and anything* from a different time unless absolutely necessary. It was a very simple rule ….

She forced her focus back to the door. *"Öffnen Vindulvian!"* she whispered, remembering the spell for opening doors, and though it shouldn't have come as a surprise (considering all the practicing she'd done), Libby gawked in astonishment as the door creaked open.

Her success would have been thrilling under other circumstances—her very first practical application outside the *Liberté!*—but she didn't have time to celebrate. Libby slipped into the darkness and shut the door behind her.

From where she crouched, she heard the voices come closer to the tower, then stop just outside the door. But why had they stopped? Had anyone seen her? Perhaps the little girl had already reported that a stranger had chased her through the streets, considered Libby ....

And what about Ginny and Esmerelda? Were they safe?

Libby held her breath as she peered into the pitch black, straining to hear anything that might give her a clue as to what was going on, though of course she couldn't understand anything being said. But then another voice cut through the darkness. *This* voice was much, much closer—just inches away, in fact—and the two words spoken made Libby's hair stand on end:

"Liberty Frye?" the voice said.

3

ᴛHE ᴍEANING ᴏF EVERYTHING

he sound of her name hung in the darkness. It was like one of those moments when you wake in the middle of the night when all the lights are off—even your cozy little nightlight (and even the one down the hallway)—and for those first few seconds, it feels as if your eyes aren't actually open, because you can't see a thing, and since you are already confused because you just woke up for no good reason, you aren't actually sure if your eyes *are* open or if you're still just dreaming ….

For Libby, it felt *just like that*, only much, much scarier.

"He-hello?"

For a moment, nothing could be heard except the sound of shifting feet beside her, which did nothing to calm Libby's nerves. She whipped her head from left to right while squinting into the dark, willing herself to make out some shape, some form, some *something* ....

"Are you Liberty Frye?"

That voice again. Barely a whisper, but in Libby's ears, it blared like a foghorn.

"Y-yes!" she stuttered back. "Who are you?"

But as soon as Libby asked the question, she realized she already knew the answer. "You-you're the girl I was chasing!" she gasped, recognizing the girl's high-pitched voice and accent. "How did you get in here?"

Footsteps beside her again, this time stepping away. Libby caught her breath, afraid to say anything more lest the girl run away, but at the same time, it was extremely unnerving to be standing in an ancient tower in the pitch dark with a total stranger ....

"There is a tunnel," came the girl's voice in reply. It was so quiet. "I can show you the way so you are not seen ...." The girl paused, as if thinking something over before adding, "You do not wish to be seen here, is that not so?"

Libby nodded, barely believing her ears. "Yes."

"You must first tell me why," returned the girl. "I must first understand your predicament before coming to your aid; that is my offer. Do you accept?"

"Do I have any choice?"

Just then, the voices from outside grew louder, followed by the metallic squeak of the door's ring.

"Fine!" Libby agreed in a rush. "What do you want to know?"

More squeaking from outside, and now the thump of someone's weight against the door. But why hadn't it opened already?

"Please!" Libby urged.

"Come."

A small hand encircled her wrist and tugged her forward. Libby jerked—probably at the prospect of more bite-marks— but still, the girl's grip felt oddly familiar, as if she'd already been here before, as if she and this strange little girl had done this exact thing more than once ....

Libby blinked uselessly into the dark as she stumbled after the girl, her free hand feeling along the cold, damp stones.

They were moving surprisingly fast, and soon they were crawling through what must be a narrow passageway. Libby's muscles burned and the air grew thicker; it smelled of wet earth and something akin to rust, and as she scuttled behind the girl, her moonstone necklace thumped against her sternum with each movement, like a pendulum keeping time.

"Stop!"

Libby nearly slammed into the girl.

"We will wait here," the girl whispered.

Libby nodded and sank to the damp floor, panting. She leaned against the tunnel wall, too tired to care what might be crawling in the darkness.

"It is time for you to fulfill your obligation. Do this, and I will show you the rest of the way."

Libby took more deep breaths and then swallowed. She was so thirsty.

CHAPTER 3

"Are you listening to me, Liberty Frye?"

Libby shook herself. "Right," she blurted. "What is it you want to know? And …," she managed between gulps of air, "could you at least tell me your name?"

Another pause. This was getting irritating. But then Libby heard the girl shift. She could feel her leaning toward her, though in the darkness she still could not see her shape. Even so, she felt her nearness in the same way you can feel static electricity, the way it pulls at your skin, drawing the hairs on your arms up and out ….

For some reason, to Libby, it suddenly felt very hard to breathe.

"My name is Ine," the girl finally said.

"Een-a," Libby repeated the pronunciation, almost in relief. If she couldn't see who she was speaking to, at least she knew her name.

"And I want to know …."

"Yes?"

The girl shifted again.

"I want to know *everything.*"

But it turns out *everything* is a slippery concept. For instance, considered Libby, if she actually knew *everything*, then she wouldn't be in the predicament she now found herself in. She'd already be back home in Baluhla, Mississippi, snug in her room, enjoying a good book and possibly even a hot chocolate.

Or was it daytime there? Well, if so, then she'd probably be outside … or maybe at school. She'd almost forgotten about school. It had been so long since she'd done anything a normal eleven-year-old would do that she'd nearly forgotten what a day back home was like. But then again, if she knew *everything*, there would be no need for school, would there?

As Libby sat in the darkness of the tunnel, random thoughts about *everything* banged about in her head as if they could somehow drum out the guilt she felt—that heavy, dragging feeling deep inside—because just moments before, she had done the One Thing She Should Never Ever Do:

She'd broken the rules of time travel and told Ine everything.

She hadn't meant to. She'd tried using some lame explanations as to why she and Ginny and Esmerelda had arrived on the shores of Qingdao, China, in such a strange manner. But Ine had apparently already seen the *Liberté* in the harbor, and anyway, providing an alternative—yet believable— explanation for a robot and two displaced strangers sneaking onto shore in pursuit of local clothing is actually a very difficult thing to do ….

Finally, they were moving again. Soon, Libby squeezed through an opening; she felt like a fish swimming toward a sunlit surface, only in this case, the surface was hazy with mist filtering the moonlight beyond so the sky glowed with weak, grey light. And then she breathed in deep gulps of air.

"This way," whispered Ine, turning down a path. Her pale hair glowed strangely in the filtered moonlight, but then she flipped the hood of her cape over her head, making all but her bare legs and sandaled feet nearly invisible.

Once more Libby followed, eager to get back to the *Liberté* and leave this fishing village behind. Quite frankly, she was eager to leave Ine behind, to forget this night ever happened. Surely, all the things she'd told Ine would come to nothing. Maybe this strange little girl would wake up the next morning and think this had all been a dream.

"We're here."

Libby skidded to a stop, nearly falling into a pool of mud in the process, overcome with that same, strange feeling of *déjà vu* she'd had earlier that evening, as if this moment had happened before ….

Libby peered through the misty air. She could barely make out the water beyond—the night was that foggy—but then she heard Ginny yelping out her name, and in the next moment she saw her best friend running toward her from the general direction of where their rowboat must be.

"There you are!" Ginny puffed, her eyes flicking over Libby's soggy pants and mud-caked boots as she stopped by the puddle.

"Ginny, thank goodness you're okay! But where's Esmerelda? And where's the woman?"

Ginny waved an impatient hand. "The woman left as soon as you took off. It's Uncle Frank we've got to worry about—he's gone looking for you! Esmerelda went back to the ship to tell him what happened, and then he just sort of lost it. He used his hover vent to leave the *Liberté*, I guess, and next thing

I know, I see our rowboat show up with him in it! He told me to stay put while he searches for you and I—"

"You mean he's out here right now?" interrupted Libby, panicked. "Just wandering around in his mobile unit?"

"Exactly!" agreed Ginny. "I mean, if he uses the spider-leg function around here, people will freak! It's weird enough where we come from!"

But then a low whirring sound distracted them both, and in the next minute an elderly man with wild, curly hair appeared through the mist. He sat in a robotic chair with all sorts of vents and buttons sticking out in random places.

"Girls!" shouted Uncle Frank, his eyes darting between Libby and Ginny, then to the foggy shore. He didn't seem to notice Ine. "Get into the rowboat this instant! We're headed back to the *Liberté* and then we're going upriver! We've no time to waste!"

4

THE THING UNDERNEATH

The *Liberté* skimmed through the water like a gigantic insect, the hum of her engine rattling over the misty river.

Libby and Ginny peered from the ship's windows, seeing nothing but the faint touch of moonlight along the bank. Uncle Frank and Sal didn't dare use any lights. It was bad enough they had to resort to their engine, but due to the lack of wind they hadn't really any choice.

At least Esmerelda could use her infrared sight, and she commanded with full authority from their captain's cabin below deck. (It was a fortunate thing, too, because at one point the river unexpectedly forked into two, with an island in between, and had Esmerelda not spotted the churning rapids and waterfall on the right, they very well could have taken the wrong side.)

Libby's brain still buzzed from all that had happened that evening, starting with the woman who'd appeared out of nowhere with the bundle of clothes. From there, things had gone from strange to downright bizarro before Uncle Frank showed up on shore, demanding they get back to their ship. He'd been in such a flurry that Libby never had a chance to say goodbye to Ine. He'd practically shoved them into the rowboat, the whole time muttering things under his breath that neither Libby nor Ginny could understand. Not that they understood what Uncle Frank was saying under normal circumstances, but still, there's a big difference between an enthusiastic muttering genius and an agitated one, so they'd sat in silence while rowing back to the *Liberté*, not daring to upset him further.

It wasn't until now—when they'd safely slipped from the fishing harbor and made their way up a river obscured by willow trees—that Libby finally asked the question that had been nagging at her all night:

"What about the old woman who met us on the shore?"

She sidled up to her great uncle with a cup of tea sweetened with palm sugar, and stared gloomily at its steamy surface. She missed her hot cocoa so much. For that matter, she missed *anything* made of chocolate. It wasn't that chocolate didn't exist in 1871, but it wasn't exactly something a person could find while sailing across the ocean.

And although her spell-making was improving, it turns out chocolate is a tricky thing to recreate. Even with the help of her spell book and the extra notes Sabine had inserted between the pages, the closest Libby had gotten was a murky concoction that was too sour and soggy to eat by itself and too lumpy to dissolve in a beverage. Not to mention the odor. Even Sal had refused to try it. For some reason, this thought made Libby's stomach growl.

"You haven't had supper, have you, kiddo?" Uncle Frank harrumphed, studying her from under his bushy brows. "There are some biscuits in the galley still. You and Ginny should have them, then off to bed."

Libby tried not to roll her eyes at the thought of eating chalky, tasteless biscuits for another night. It felt like forever since they'd had a decent meal, but now was not the time to discuss their pathetic culinary options. So instead she took a sip of her tea, which, incidentally, made her feel rather grown up. And at this particular moment, that's exactly the feeling she needed.

"Sure." She watched Uncle Frank closely. "Just as soon as you tell me what this is all about. I mean, that lady was helping us. So why are we hiding upriver now?"

Ginny turned from her perch by the window. "Libby's right! The whole idea was to get some clothes and then set out on our journey tomorrow, right? And then that lady appeared with the exact items we were looking for, so *someone* sent her to help …."

"Well, that's just it, kid," cut in Sal. He'd been at the wheel with Esmerelda, remaining uncharacteristically silent the whole evening. "When Essie came back to tell us what happened, it became clear we needed to beat feet. It's obvious!"

Libby glanced over at Ginny, but she looked equally confused. "What's ... er, *obvious?*"

"The trap, Libby," Uncle Frank practically spat in reply. "We're not exactly inconspicuous here, now, are we? We must have been spotted hours before you, Ginny and Esmerelda went ashore—"

"Which of course gives the suspicious sort plenty of time to develop a plan," added Sal. He pursed his lips. "It doesn't take the work of a wizard to see a fancy foreign ship and guess it must be here for *some* reason. Now, if you were the cunning kind, wouldn't you take advantage of that? Wouldn't you try to think of a way to get your hands on whatever this ship must be carrying?"

Libby thought about that as she took another sip of tea, hoping it might douse the sudden uneasiness gurgling up her throat. Because, of course. It *was* obvious:

They'd landed in a tiny fishing village where the *Liberté* stood out like the Empire State Building. And in the minds of almost anyone here, it would appear that such a ship must have fabulous treasures: gold, precious stones, silks (they *did* have lots of silk, incidentally) and exotic goods. Things that could make a person—no, that could make an entire village—rich beyond their wildest dreams ....

"So Sal and I decided to begin our mountain trek from a more secluded spot," concluded Uncle Frank. "We should be a bit closer to the foothills if we continue upriver anyway."

"But what about that girl?" persisted Ginny. "*She* didn't seem part of any plan, did she, Libby? She was scared out of her mind! She took off as soon as we spotted her!"

"But what about later?"

"Huh?"

"Later," Libby repeated. "When the girl found me in the tower and helped me back to the harbor? You saw her, right before Uncle Frank showed up!"

"*I* didn't see any kid," muttered Uncle Frank.

Ginny chewed her lip in obvious agitation as she blinked between Uncle Frank and Libby, and for several seconds, no one said another word. "From now on," she eventually declared, her voice taking an odd, tight tone, "I think we definitely need to stick together."

"Agreed," said Uncle Frank. "Libby?"

Libby nodded as she looked back at her great uncle, hoping he'd see that she understood. Hoping he'd relax. He was acting so strange of late. And her worst fear was that he'd keel over with a heart attack before they ever reached home. Over the past two months, she had tried to help, to replenish the various teas and tinctures her mom used to make for him, but there were only certain spells she felt comfortable using, and a spell to mess with Uncle Frank's depleted meds wasn't one of them.

Granted, all in all, the journey actually seemed to have done Uncle Frank some good. He looked invigorated. Some days, he even appeared younger. But there was no denying his condition … or the fact that while he might *look* younger from time to time, he certainly wasn't *getting* younger.

"I'm sorry," she added quietly. "I shouldn't have run after the girl. From now on, I'll stick to the plan."

That seemed to help. Uncle Frank even smiled a little,

sending deep crinkles along the edges of his eyes and down through his cheeks. When Uncle Frank smiled like that, it made Libby feel like she was back at his rundown old mansion in the woods. She missed everything about that crumbling house. She missed her parents being there with them; she missed her dad growing exasperated and her mom laughing and Uncle Frank shouting his insistence about some new scientific theory. How could it be that life used to be so wonderful? So safe? So … ordinary?

Uncle Frank ruffled her hair at the top of her head, the way her dad used to when she was younger. "I think we can all learn from this experience." He harrumphed. "But what we need to focus on *now* is our choices going forward. And our next choice should be to get some sleep. We're no good to each other if we're exhausted and irritable. So off to bed, you two."

Libby glanced into his face as he said those words, and despite that warmth in his eyes and those crinkles around them, this time she caught a look of something else deeper within. A flicker. A *fear*. And not just any fear. This one felt distinctly personal, like the way she'd sometimes seen her parents glancing at her when her mom's health started getting worse ….

The realization tickled a thought somewhere deep in her mind. A possibility she couldn't fully comprehend. Not yet. But it was there, wiggling its tail under the soft folds of her brain. Itching. Scratching. Struggling to become *more* ….

Now that she'd realized it, she knew:

Whatever it was, it was *there*.

And soon, it would come out.

5

Of Magic and Mirrors

The next morning, Libby awoke with the unaccountable sensation that she'd slept through something important.

"Ginny?" she called.

Nothing came in reply.

She shivered and scuttled to the edge of her bed, grabbing her necklace off a hook on her bunk post and slipping the titanium chain over her head. The blue and wispy white moonstone fell with a heavy *thunk* against her skin, but she was so used to it by now that she hardly noticed its weight.

Libby pulled out a tattered, long-sleeve shirt she'd folded in a box underneath the bunk. The boxes served as their make-shift dressers, and, thanks to the abundance of silk they'd been allotted from Captain Hayes's pirate ship, they still had clothes on their backs, thank goodness … although most of the silk hadn't been used for clothes at all, but rather stitched together into giant sheets for some enigmatic reason that Uncle Frank refused to divulge.

"Semper paratus!" Libby muttered gruffly, using her best Uncle Frank voice.

This more or less translated to "always be prepared" in Latin, and it was a phrase Uncle Frank loved to declare on a near-daily basis—especially, Libby had learned, when they were stuck on a ship in the middle of the ocean.

For two months they'd filled their days with cleaning; food preparation; lectures on marine life, navigation and history; and—of course—sewing. When Libby and Ginny had asked why they were sewing together sheets of silk, Uncle Frank would just grin and then shout, *"Semper paratus!"*

Libby hurriedly threw on some long pants and headed to the galley. It was her turn to cook breakfast, and she'd planned a special treat for everyone this morning: pancakes with reconstituted dried bananas, shredded coconut and palm syrup. She'd be using the last of their dried bananas, but since they were finally at their destination she figured it was the perfect way to celebrate.

And then, as soon as Libby turned the corner into the galley, all thoughts of pancakes flew out the window. Or rather, out the cabin door because Libby noticed it was flung open. Sunshine spilled over the teak floors and gleaming countertop, and Esmerelda sat at the dining booth, eyes closed as she recharged, but otherwise the cabin was empty.

A spooky feeling crept through her stomach. It was so quiet in here. It was so quiet *out there*.

Without thinking, Libby turned to the stairs. She took the first step, noticing now that Buttercup snoozed in the shadows beside the stairway, his head tucked under his left wing. She took the next step, the strange churning in her gut growing stronger. Third step. Fourth step. Sunlight blared through the open doorway so that she squinted into the brightness, blinded by it. Fifth step. Almost there. She didn't know what was happening; she didn't know why she felt the way she did; she didn't know what she expected to find on the deck that should make her feel this way; she didn't know anything but this:

She knew whatever happened next would change *everything*.

And it did.

Libby stood on the ship deck, staring at the riverbank before her. There, four men silently stared back, as if waiting. And from their demeanor together with a banner that fluttered overhead, it was obvious *who* they were waiting for.

"No!" she whispered.

"I know," murmured Ginny.

"But how …?"

"They were here when I came on deck this morning," said Sal. "Who knows how long they've been waiting."

"But we—"

"I know," repeated Ginny, nodding furiously. "It's impossible."

Impossible.

That word again.

What else in her life had been impossible?

So many things.

As if the *impossible* had more often than not become quite the opposite. Hadn't the old woman summed it up last night? What was it she'd said?

"Yes," whispered Libby, still staring, stunned, at the four men on the riverbank. She remembered now:

"Isn't the impossible why you are here, Liberty Frye?"

That's *exactly* what that old woman had said.

And that's exactly what was happening now.

"The Wizard sent them. There's no other explanation," said Ginny. Her eyes remained locked on the banner.

"That would be the most logical conclusion," said Uncle Frank, his voice controlled and low. "Libby," he continued, though his gaze never left the shore, "please go downstairs and wake Esmerelda. I think we'll be requiring her translation services."

Libby felt too rattled to question much of anything, so she turned numbly to the stairs and made her way back down to the galley. When she got there, she found Esmerelda still seated at the booth, perfect posture, eyelids closed. Buttercup remained sleeping in the shadows.

It was uncanny.

Another one of those moments.

Down here, one would never guess that just several feet above, another reality awaited. A reality where four strangers stood on the riverbank, calmly watching the *Liberté*. Waiting.

A reality where a platform-like carriage—the perfect size

for carrying Uncle Frank in his mobile unit—rested on the ground among those four men.

A reality where, impossibly, a cloth banner fluttered from the carriage top … bearing these letters in bold, black ink:

LIBERTY FRYE

Down here, reality was familiar. It was expected. It didn't jangle the mind or send flittering wings through the gut. It was *normal.*

Down here, reality was exactly how Libby had left things not five minutes before.

Except that it wasn't.

"Good morning!"

Libby spun around, shocked out of her wits. Then she blinked at the sight of a little girl with blonde hair standing before her. Libby opened her mouth, but her questions were knitted so tightly in the jumble of her mind that none could loosen themselves into a sentence.

Because even in a world as unlikely as Libby's, *this* didn't make any sense. But she knew she wasn't dreaming; she'd just run all the usual checks: pinching, blinking, coughing … pretty much anything one can do that proves one is awake. And not crazy.

"What are *you* doing here?" she finally managed to say.

"I am here," Ine briskly replied, "to help you on your journey. I should think that would be obvious. Did you not tell me just last night that you are in search of the Wizard? Is that not why you are here? Are those not the mountains in the distance that are rumored to enshroud him? Everyone here knows about the Wizard, Liberty Frye. I, for one, would very much like to actually *meet* him."

"But we left you at the shore last night!"

"Again, a fairly obvious observation ...."

"But how did you ...?"

"You are not the only one with a vessel," replied Ine with impatience. "Goodness! I thought you would be pleased!"

"And-and," continued Libby in a splutter, because the most random thoughts and questions were untangling themselves all at once, "why are you even speaking like this? You're *German!* And you're so *young!*"

Ine shrugged. "My mother teaches languages. I am an excellent student."

Libby swallowed hard. "That actually makes sense," she finally said, but her brain throbbed and felt stuffed with cotton, all at the same time.

"But ...," she continued, determined to find the question she should actually be asking, "how did you *get here?* We traveled all night!"

Ine shrugged again. "I happen to have rather a lot of experience with boats. I simply followed you. It was easy. The fog obliged in making me invisible to you, and due to your uncle's ... um, infirmity ...," she paused to throw a quizzical glance around the cabin where all sorts of Uncle Frank's inventions lay evident: distillers, compressors, solar-powered machines, new walkie-talkies shining and ready for their

mountain journey, some sort of propeller engine on the floor …,
"I had time enough to slip aboard while you three were still
disembarking from the rowboat."

Libby felt her eyelids spasm. This didn't help matters. She
felt discombobulated by this strange girl who kept showing up
in the most unexpected places. "But your parents …."

"My father is away, and my mother will simply assume I am
staying at my friend Liling's home. Now, come. You cannot
expect that creature to interpret for you!" Ine threw a
distrustful scowl Esmerelda's way. "You have caused enough
of a stir as it is; I am sure our village elders have called a search
for your ship and are scouring the rivers as we speak. There is
little time to waste."

Little time to waste.

There it was again: that concept of time. *We always talk
about it,* thought Libby randomly. She knew she was still
standing there, still as a statue, eyes blinking. She was standing
still, but time was wasting away. *We always talk about it, but what
is it? What is it really?*

"It's like money," she whispered, too numb to know she'd
said it out loud.

"I beg your pardon?"

"T-time," sputtered Libby, and the sound of her voice
seemed to help her brain better grapple with what was
happening. "It's like this thing we measure and use and
exchange, like money. It … it controls everything. Except we
can't see it. Or make it. Or own it. It's something so important
to everyone, but no one knows what it *is.* How is that possible?"

Ine regarded her with her grey-blue eyes. To Libby, the girl's eyes were like mirrors—wide and serene and silvery. But also the crafty kind, like mirrors at carnivals: impossible to see through, hiding things Libby didn't understand, reflecting things she couldn't recognize.

The kind that play tricks.

Several seconds ticked by in silence. Then a whole minute. Libby felt dizzy standing there, staring back at this girl with the silvery, solemn eyes.

"Time," Ine replied softly. A twitch lifted the left corner of her mouth. "I suppose it is akin to magic."

6

The Girl Who Wasn't

Nearly three hours had come and gone since Ine made her surprise appearance aboard the *Liberté*. And despite Libby's explanation when she'd brought Ine on deck to meet everyone, Ginny still couldn't believe any of this was actually happening. It was bad enough that a strange little girl had stowed away on their ship, but the real problem lay in what happened next:

Somehow, that pesky girl had managed to join the expedition up the mountain ... and yet, Ginny had been instructed to stay behind. So had Sal, Esmerelda and Buttercup, incidentally, but that didn't count. Not really.

From where she stood on the ship deck, Ginny scowled furiously at the mountains, at the spot where she'd last seen

Ine, Uncle Frank, Libby and the four men, right before they'd dissolved into specks in the distance. And instead of her anger cooling over time, with each minute that passed, she only grew more indignant.

How could they?

How *dare* they leave her behind?

Ginny's bones shook inside her skin. Her blood roiled. Her eyes narrowed into slits leaking tears so hot, they practically evaporated. On. The. Spot.

"STUPID!" she finally screamed in their general direction. "After EVERYTHING we agreed to, you go and do something like THIS? What is WRONG with you?"

There was no denying the sound of Ginny's words. They were direct. They were very, very loud. Perhaps even the mountains heard them. And even to someone who might not speak English, the wrath behind them was definite.

"Ginny," Sal said, looking up from the sheets of silk he'd hauled to the deck, "you need to calm down."

"CALM DOWN?" If possible, her words grew even louder. "You want *me* to *calm down* when my best friend and my Uncle Frank—he's my uncle, too, you know! It's official since I'm part of the family, so don't try arguing otherwise!—go up a flinging mountain with total strangers? And leave *us* behind?"

"I agree, it seems—"

"*Us!* They leave *us* behind when this whole time, after *everything* we've been through, the one thing we could agree on, the *ONE THING* we've promised each other is to stick together!"

"I know—"

"We *PROMISED* each other!"

"It's not—Oh, Ginny. Come on, kid. You've got to calm down!"

But Ginny couldn't calm down. Sobs exploded out of her, fountains, mountains of feelings that her tears barely expressed. There simply wasn't enough water. She shook so hard she fell over, and she would have smashed against the deck had Sal not caught her in time. Even then, she couldn't stop crying. She sobbed and sobbed like a baby, lying on the deck where Sal held her.

It was awkward. For Sal, at least.

He wasn't used to holding children of any sort, much less Ginny. He didn't know what to do, but he couldn't exactly extract himself. Ginny's arms and hands were wrapped around him so tight ….

Well, it was shocking, to be honest. He hadn't known she was that strong.

"AHH-ARG!" gurgled Ginny, because there was nothing else to say.

Sal sat on the deck, tangled with a tear-spouting, snot-oozing, spit-spittled girl. He marveled at just how *much* could come out of something so relatively small. Then he tried patting her head. What a ridiculous thing to do.

"Why would they leave me?" she finally whimpered. "How could they do that? We're supposed to be in this *together!*"

"We're still in this together, kid. They'll only be gone a few days."

"You don't understand!" moaned Ginny, hiccupping between her tears.

Well, Sal had to agree with that, at least. He definitely didn't understand.

"You don't know what it's like …. And I-I worry!"

Sal nodded; he worried, too. He'd been there when that peculiar blonde girl came on deck with Libby. There when Libby explained who she was and how she'd come to be on their ship. There when the girl began translating for them, there when she explained the four men waiting on the riverbank claimed to be sent by the Wizard. Why? The four men did not know why. They did not question such things. It was simply a great honor to be of service, and that was that. It was an honor alone to be sought out, to have one's existence even known by the Wizard. Their eyes trembled with awe and expectation as they turned their gazes upon Libby and Uncle Frank.

To actually see the Wizard, they'd uttered in hushed, fervent tones, *for the Wizard to choose to reveal himself to the two of them? That was an honor of unimaginable proportions. Do you not know,* they'd concluded, *that the Wizard has the power to make himself invisible? And he has remained so … for centuries.*

So, yes: Sal definitely felt unsettled. He didn't like the idea of Frank and Libby taking off with that girl and those four men, either.

But those had been the conditions.

Or at least that is what the men had claimed.

Or, at the very least, that is what Ine had translated ….

A cold burn traveled up Sal's ribs, and it wasn't from the uncomfortable position he found himself locked in. He grimaced over the top of Ginny's hot, soggy head. Come to think of it, perhaps they should have gotten a second opinion before all of this foolishness. Hang what the locals might think about Esmerelda; they should have wakened her. As if they hadn't already caused a flurry; as if the families belonging to those four men didn't already suspect something *very strange* was happening.

After all, you don't just wake up in the morning and kiss your family members goodbye with explanations that you're off to see the Wizard ....

That would just be weird.

No, they would have *explained*. Surely, they would have mentioned the foreign ship. Surely, news of the *Liberté's* unusual arrival had spread throughout the region by now. Hadn't Libby already been chased by some of the villagers last night? And hadn't they been approached by perfect strangers twice now: once by the woman last night and then by the four men this morning?

Nope, the cat was already out of the bag, so to speak. So much for stealthy arrivals ....

"The-the last time we were separated," Ginny blubbered into Sal's sleeve, "really bad things happened. It's what started this whole mess! That's when Libby's parents were drugged and Libby was kidnapped, and-and—"

"And Libby turned into a witch?" finished Sal. He was only trying to help.

"She di-didn't *turn into* a witch," said Ginny between hiccups. "Sh-she always was one, I guess, but still, if she'd just stayed in Mississippi, she could have been a happy witch.

She wouldn't have ever even met Zelna. None of the awful things that have happened would have happened!"

"Got ya," said Sal. He was beginning to understand. "And now, you're afraid that since they've left again, something horrible will take place, right?"

"Something horrible is *already* happening," wailed Ginny, "and I'm not just talking about this whole stuck-in-the-1800s thing!"

More sobbing. Sal wasn't sure, but it sounded like Ginny had just blown her nose on his sleeve. He pressed his mouth together and forced his eyes on the mountains that rose beyond the riverbanks. Forget what those four men had claimed. Why had Frank agreed to this arrangement? And why in tarnation had he, Salvador McCool, actually *allowed* them to go?

He should have held his ground. Ginny was right; they should have all stayed together. Beyond his concern for Frank and Libby journeying up a mountain with total strangers, he had his own situations to fret over. *This* situation, for example. He didn't understand children, and he certainly didn't understand a weeping, preteen female. What on earth was he supposed to *do?*

Sal squinted through a gap in the willow trees where a motion in the far distance suddenly caught his attention. What was it? A cloud? That didn't make any sense, for it was moving along the ground, whatever it was ....

"I mean ... that girl," sputtered Ginny into his sleeve; it was sopping wet, sticking to his skin. A glue of snot and spit and tears.

He tried not to think about it. "Yep?"

"Libby said she followed us from the shore last night …"

Sal kept his eyes locked on the motion in the distance. He should get his telescope. But how to untangle himself from Ginny?

"… but I was *there*," she continued, now sniffing and raising her face. Her eyes were so swollen she could barely lift her lids enough to see. "I was *right there* before Uncle Frank showed up. I was *talking* to Libby!"

"Shh, it's okay, kid." Sal patted her hair again, distracted by the cloud that wasn't a cloud in the distance.

Ginny scrambled to her knees, then grabbed Sal by the arms, forcing him to look into her swollen, splotched face. "I'm saying I was standing right there! Libby and me! And that's it!"

Sal's forehead scrunched into rows of Vs. "What are getting at, kid?"

"I'm saying that girl … Ine, isn't that her name? Well, she *wasn't.*"

"Wasn't *what,* kid?"

Ginny stared hard at Sal, slits of brown barely slicing through the ping-pong swell of her eyelids. Her fingers dug into his arms.

"Ine was on board today; we all saw her, obviously. Right?"

Sal nodded. He was afraid to say anything else lest Ginny grow even more agitated. And his arms were starting to hurt under her grip. This girl was *strong.*

"And she claimed she'd followed us last night from the harbor. Libby said it, too. Right?"

Sal gulped and then nodded again. He needed to work on his calisthenics. Obviously, he was losing muscle tone. It felt like her fingers were digging straight into his bones ....

"But I was there last night at the harbor." Ginny spoke slowly now, deliberately. Each word chosen with care. And with every syllable, her fingers dug harder into Sal's arms. "I was *there* when we first arrived on the shore. I was *there* when the old woman appeared with the clothes and *there* when that Ine girl stood up from where she'd been hiding and ran away. I was there when Libby ran after her like an idiot. I was *still* there when Libby came back. I was *there*, talking to Libby before Uncle Frank showed up—we were standing by a puddle a few feet from the shore—and I am absolutely, 100-percent positive about this ...."

"What, Ginny?" Sal gasped. He couldn't help it. His arms were killing him.

"I'm saying that Ine wasn't there!"

7

(THE EXPEDITION

Granite and grass rose before them.

To Libby, it felt as if the expedition would go on forever. The craggy silhouette of the mountains towered ahead, and if she turned around, she could see the river twist its way to the harbor in the distance, to the little fishing village where, by now, news of the *Liberté's* disappearance was sure to have caused a stir.

The air carried a whip in its hand—chilly gusts that cut through her tunic—but sunlight warmed the rocks and paused over mountain springs, transforming the latter into glittering, emerald pools. At times they passed trees with leaves turned to gold, and when the sun glowed through these, the trees dazzled and danced, their leaves whispering in the wind.

Also, there was a scream. It shook the air and latched itself to the wind, forcing its sound out and out and out: *"S-T-U-P-I-D!"*

Libby chewed her lower lip, but it didn't squash the worry away. Or the guilt. It wasn't that she felt she'd abandoned Ginny and the rest to hopeless doom—after all, it was far safer for them to wait on the ship, hidden by trees, than to trek through a mountain wilderness—but she'd known Ginny long enough to understand that her best friend had some serious abandonment issues. And with good reason.

She peeked up at Uncle Frank, hoping to catch his reaction. Did he feel guilt? Worry? It was impossible to tell. Uncle Frank was a mask of pinched lips and wide eyes.

It was odd to travel like this, hiking alongside four strangers who touted a bamboo carriage on their shoulders. On that carriage, of course, sat Uncle Frank in his mobile unit. Libby thought he looked ridiculous, but of course she didn't say so. Anyway, from the scowl on his face, she was sure he already felt that way.

"Poor Ginny," she said instead.

Uncle Frank grimaced. "We hadn't any choice, kiddo. These are the terms the Wizard insisted upon. I don't like it any more than you ...."

Libby nodded. She didn't know what else to say. So she turned to the mountainside before them.

According to what the four men had told Ine, it would take all day and part of tomorrow to get there. If there actually was a *there*. She was starting to have doubts. Granted, something beyond their scope of understanding was *definitely* going on.

The old woman waiting for them last night, for instance, and then the four men this morning ....

She glanced down at her tunic, then to her wide trousers (they were long enough to hide her trusty boots, thank goodness), all items from the sack of clothes the woman had brought. And Libby had a belt around her waist with an embroidered satchel hanging from it, too. This contained the contents from her backpack and one of the walkie-talkies Uncle Frank had made for their journey. Her long hair was pulled back and tucked under the neck of her tunic, and on her head she wore a twisted pile of cloth that Ine had arranged in the local fashion. Who they would meet on their way to the mountain that should require such a disguise was beyond her, but in any case, all this preparation made it seem as if the Wizard really had anticipated their every move, as if he were somehow *watching* them.

Which brought up a peculiar question ....

"But why," she said, turning once more to Uncle Frank; she studied the blanket thrown over his mobile unit, then the costume he'd donned from the sack of clothes, "would the Wizard have sent that woman to meet us if he'd known we'd be going upriver anyway? Why go to the trouble? Why not have the men waiting with these clothes and skip the woman altogether?"

It occurred to her that this should have been the type of question asked *before* they agreed to head out. With total strangers. Up a remote mountain. Where an invisible Wizard waited ....

"Imagine if he hadn't sent the woman," replied Uncle Frank after a moment, his tone thoughtful, soft. There was even a hint of admiration somewhere in there. "Then what? All sorts of potential results might have occurred. We could have gotten lost. Arrested. Who knows? Perhaps by sending the woman, he anticipated what our reaction would be, thereby placing us in the position he actually *wanted* us to be in. Ergo, the riverbank this morning ...."

Libby's head swam. Since they'd hit land less than twenty-four hours ago, everything had turned upside down. Real was fake and out was in ... or something along those lines. She had no idea what was going on, and their blonde-haired companion wasn't exactly helping matters. In fact, ever since Libby and Uncle Frank had agreed to come on this mountain trek, Ine had been acting very strangely. *Well, relatively strangely,* Libby mentally amended. *For her.*

Maybe the girl was still miffed at Uncle Frank, who had at first insisted she return home immediately. Then he'd begged. Finally, he'd tried bribing, but Ine wasn't having it. Sal had even offered to sail the *Liberté* back down the river and drop Ine somewhere near her village, but Ine had scoffed at them all.

"I find it perplexing," she had said, "that the *one person* who has truly helped you—that would be me, incidentally—is the one person you are trying to send away!"

"Because you're a little kid!" Ginny had snapped.

But no amount of arguing could persuade Ine to go home. Finally, she'd just climbed down to their rowboat and sat there with crossed arms until Libby and Uncle Frank joined her.

Libby still remembered the expression on Ginny's face. At first it was disbelief. And then …

Betrayal.

Hurt.

Anger.

They'd *promised* ….

Without thinking, Libby curled her arms around her middle. She looked again to the mountain rising ahead, then to where Ine strode several feet in front.

Why was she here?

Libby glimpsed down at her hand, but just as she did so, she noticed the most curious thing: Her hand—the same hand she'd used last night to catch Ine when she'd chased her through the village streets; the same hand that Ine had sunk her teeth into—that *same hand* showed no bite marks at all!

Libby froze mid-step.

"What is it?" called Uncle Frank.

"Uh—" Libby glanced from her hand to the back of Ine's head, then up at Uncle Frank. Was she crazy? Maybe those two months on the ship really had messed with her mind. Was it possible she'd just imagined the bite marks? Or had they just … *disappeared?*

"Nothing," she muttered, resuming her pace.

But as she followed Ine, a whole new set of questions tumbled through her brain. *When had she last examined her hand? Were the marks there this morning, before they'd left? Had she even looked? What about last night, before she'd gone to bed?* She couldn't remember.

They continued on, and soon the gentle beauty of the mountain grew more and more wild. The wind lashed its gale through the granite pass they'd just reached, the tall grey slabs of stone standing stark against the green. The world was saturated, doused in color and wind and … energy.

Libby closed her eyes as the wind whipped through her. She breathed it in. It felt as if there was so much energy, she might explode from it. And that she might laugh and cry and dance and scream, all at once. *What is wrong with me?*

Libby opened her eyes and glared at the ground, determined to steady her thinking. Her arms clenched tighter around her middle. She needed to focus. They were on a mission, after all, and considering how far they'd come to get here, the last thing she needed to do was unravel.

The sun danced over rocks and glowed against the grass. It glowed over the moss carpeting the edges of granite. The sun darted and swiveled; it was everywhere, in every direction: it shone up and through and down and over. It was here and there. It twinkled in her memory from an hour ago, yet it was here, shining still, just as real, just as vibrant. And it was *warm*, the kind of warmth you recognize at once, different than, say, freshly baked bread. Different than a hot bath. Different, even, from her mother's hug ….

The warmth centered over her. It radiated and throbbed. The warmth, so comforting at first, started to burn, and then, before she knew what was happening ….

"Libby!" bellowed Uncle Frank, turning so forcefully toward her that he almost fell out of his mobile unit. The four men stopped. They exchanged glances, confused. Ine turned as well, her eyes pools of interest.

"Libby, kiddo, take it off! Take it off *this instant!*"

Take what off? What is he yelling about?

The ground beneath her feet glowed. The wind whipped sharply now, clearing right though her skin, ripping through eyes and bone and sinew; it was nothing, all nothing but … energy. What a waste. What a waste it had all been until now.

The granite rose up and around; it seemed to grow by the second, rising under her feet, shuddering into walls stretching for the sky, grey and rich and packed with matter. It vibrated and hummed, the shell of something *so much more* within, practically exploding to liquid. Practically grafting to her skin. And, oh, the energy. There was *so much* of it ….

"Libby, stop it! Take it *OFF!*"

She blinked. Uncle Frank was on the ground, his legs splayed limp behind him, his hands clutched at her tunic.

"Uncle Frank, what are you doing?"

His hands pulled at her tunic, willing themselves up, up, up, like feet on a ladder.

"Please, kiddo," his voice broke, and the sound of it shattered the glow all around. It was too much. But why was he upset?

"Please," he repeated, now in such a whisper that she could barely hear. But it didn't matter.

She followed his gaze and discovered her hand already clasped over the object of his attention. The moonstone. It pulsed under her touch, burning with such intensity that she suddenly cried out.

"Now, Libby!"

And the next thing she saw was a blue flame, so blue that it was white, ripping from her chest.

8

MEMORIES AND GHOSTS

From where Ginny and Sal waited on the deck of the *Liberté*, the cloud that wasn't a cloud drew nearer. And although it wasn't a *cloud*, it *was* a whirlwind; a whirlwind of dust and pounding horses' hooves and flapping capes.

Sal swiveled his telescope from the land to the river. Upstream from where they'd anchored, the river ended in a series of waterfalls tumbling from the mountains. And downstream, beyond the bend of willow trees, he could see the island in the distance where the river temporarily split in two, and to the island's left he saw the river flowing into a plummeting mass of white water churning over rocks, then disappearing somewhere below. There was nowhere for them to go but back the same way they'd arrived.

Unless ....

He lowered his telescope and climbed down the rope ladder.

"Well?" Ginny squinted up at him through swollen eyes. "What's it going to be? Plan A? Or ... Plan B?"

Sal's mouth puckered as he ran his tongue over his false teeth; he wasn't sure if he'd remembered to put them in this morning, he'd been so distracted. And sleep deprived. He looked to where Ginny and Esmerelda sat on the deck, surrounded by sheets and sheets of silk.

"Plan B."

Ginny's shoulders sagged. "I was really hoping for A."

Sal grimaced by way of agreement, then scrutinized the mountains where, somewhere, he knew Libby and Frank must be, then back to the gap between the trees where he'd first spotted the cloud that wasn't a cloud.

"Let's hope for the best. If our visitors mean no harm, then we'll stay put and keep working on those sheets. But if this gets unfriendly, then we need to head back to the harbor and figure something out."

Ginny nodded her consent, not daring to say anything for fear of it coming out as a complaint. She felt mortified by her meltdown earlier, and she was determined to make it up with a super-good attitude now. Even if that meant sealing the seams of silk sheets with some sort of nasty goop Uncle Frank had stored in jars ....

Sal paced the deck, pausing to check the bolts and latches installed at various points along the boards. "Esmerelda," he called distractedly as he wiggled one of the latches, "you should go below deck and wait this out. We'll call if anything changes."

The robot heaved what Ginny assumed was supposed to be a sigh, dropped the silk seam she'd been working on, stood up and stomped toward the cabin door. "This-constantly-having-to-hide-because-I-happen-to-be-of-an-advanced-cognizant-nature-is-really-getting-annoying!" she snapped over her shoulder. And with that she disappeared through the door.

"Well at least she doesn't have to wear a scratchy shirt," said Ginny, indicating her clothes. She and Sal had changed into some of the tunics and pants that the woman had brought them, but after wearing the equivalent of rags for two months, Ginny found the stiff, course fabric of her tunic would take some getting used to.

Sal grunted and regarded her for a long minute.

"They'll be here any moment." He glanced into the distance, where the sound of pounding hooves now reached their ears. "Just in case all heck breaks loose, I want to let you know ...." He paused to consider for a moment. "Well, I don't understand what's happening around here any more than you do," he resumed, "but in regards to what you said about that girl Ine ... if you say you saw something or *didn't* see something, then I know it is true. You've got a good head on your shoulders."

Ginny blinked up at him, surprised by this sudden turn in behavior.

"I guess what I'm trying to say is that I believe in you, kid," he continued, and Ginny could only sit there in astonishment as he spoke; she'd never heard him say so many nice things about *anyone,* much less her. She wondered if he'd taken some of Uncle Frank's remaining sleep tincture; perhaps he was having some sort of allergic reaction? Was 'Acting Warm and Fuzzy When You Are Normally a Complete Grump' a legitimate allergy? She'd have to consult their first aid manual ....

"No matter what may come at you," he was saying, oblivious to Ginny's concern, "stay true to that compass you've got inside. Okay, kid? It will guide you through life."

Ginny gulped down the balloon in her throat.

"Thanks, Sal."

It was all she could manage.

Sal nodded, then squinted once more into the distance, only now the horses and their riders could be clearly seen. Ginny turned in their direction as well, holding her hand above her eyes to shade them from the sun.

"If you had to guess, who do you suppose they might be? Some sort of government officials? Or maybe some of the villagers? *Someone* must have seen us head upriver last night ...."

The horses galloped over the ground, closer and closer, dust billowing in their wake, capes leaping like flames from their riders. And then, just as the group reached the riverbank, they pulled to a stop so sudden that the animals swayed on their legs.

The riders—three in all—swayed with their beasts. Then the rider in the middle jerked her cape from her head, revealing wild, blonde hair tangling with the wind. Her blue eyes flared, her face flushed from something much more than the rigors of the journey.

Ginny watched the woman with a sense of awe mixed with dread ....

The woman's anger spawned through the distance between them, but as for her two companions, they remained blank slates of composure. Ginny could see that the first companion was a man while the second, who sat to the back of the group on the blonde woman's right side, was a woman. The man looked in his late thirties and had long black hair pulled away from his face, his eyes alert yet calm. He carried a rifle slung across the back of his horse. But the second companion, much to Ginny's astonishment, was none other than the old lady who had brought them the clothes the night before!

Ginny squeezed her eyes shut then looked again, just to make sure she wasn't imagining things, but sure enough, under her riding cape, the old woman wore the same long scarf covering her face and head so that only her eyes were unencumbered, but the glow of those eyes was unmistakable. And now that Ginny had recovered from the initial shock of their arrival to notice such things, she recognized the old woman's stooped posture, too ....

Ginny caught her breath while the horses snorted and pawed at the ground, and for a split second she wondered if they were actually preparing to charge. Sal must have had a similar thought, because he approached the port side of the ship facing the visitors and called in an uncharacteristically chipper tone:

"Greetings! How may we be of service to you on this fine day?"

That definitely threw the blonde woman off. Confusion rippled through her eyes, her gaze flicking from Sal to the side of the ship, where *Liberté* was spelled in large, white script.

"English?"

"American," said Sal. "And you?"

This question was met with silence. The blonde woman took a deep breath, her hair still whipping in the wind.

"*I?*" she practically hissed in reply. "I am Liesel Herrmann. And I demand to know what you have done with my daughter!"

Forty minutes later, Ginny and Sal stood on the deck of the *Liberté*, watching as Liesel Herrmann and her two companions galloped toward the mountains. A heavy feeling settled into Ginny's stomach.

"Do you think she'll reach them today?"

"Doubt it," replied Sal. "From what I can see, it's too rocky up there to continue without daylight, so she'll have to stop in a few hours."

"Do you think she believed us?"

Sal tightened his lips at the question, but he didn't reply at first. Instead, he contemplated the mountains.

"Well," he eventually said, "it would have helped if Libby had answered our walkie-talkie call. Wonder what's going on up there; maybe the mountains proved too much of a barrier, even for almighty Frank's inventions …."

"Maybe."

Ginny frowned at her hands, one of which still held the walkie-talkie, that heavy feeling inside her growing heavier. Then she regarded the billows of dust from where the woman and her companions had disappeared into the distance. She felt the sudden urge to run after them, to beg them to take her with them. She glanced again at her radio, and that anxiety she'd managed to quiet earlier now reared its head.

She thought once more about the last time she and Libby had been separated. It was also the last time they'd used a walkie-talkie to speak, she remembered; it was right before Libby was kidnapped by Zelna, when Libby had radioed from Germany to tell Ginny that Mr. and Mrs. Frye had been reported dead. It was *because* of that call that Ginny had been able to alert Uncle Frank and then fly to Germany to find her best friend ….

And now, *this* time, the walkie-talkies hadn't worked at all. That feeling continued to churn inside Ginny, tumbling in her stomach. *And what about that old lady?* Ginny considered fretfully. They'd been so focused on trying to reach Libby on the radio that she'd completely forgotten to ask how the old lady knew Ine's mother, and more than that, how on earth she'd known to bring them the bundle of clothes the night before. And now, of course, it was too late to ask anyone anything.

If Ginny could have, she would have kicked herself … but she wasn't coordinated enough. This, of course, didn't help matters. She'd never felt so disgusted or more of a failure in her entire life. Despite all the care she took, all the rules she followed, all the Safety Inspection Checklists she insisted upon utilizing, none of it had made a lick of difference, and one thing she *could* have done—namely, ask the old woman who she was and how she'd known about them—she'd totally blown the opportunity. As a result, she was now separated from the only people left in the world who cared for her, and there was no way for her to reach them, to protect them, to get them back.

"What is it, kid? You look like you've seen a ghost!"

Ginny glimpsed up from the walkie-talkie. "No ghost," she said.

But as she stood there, watching the dust settle in the distance, she wondered if that was a lie. Because aren't memories ghosts in a way? She certainly felt haunted by them. Ginny thought about that as she gripped the useless walkie-talkie in her hand. Memories can't be seen, can't be proven, but are they any less real? Their ability to creep in and out of your mind, to enter dreams and daydreams, to form how you approach things and people and places ....

Their hold is unmistakable.

And at this particular moment, the ghost of things that happened in the past, things that Ginny knew should have ended very, very differently ....

That ghost had come back to stay.

9

THE ELIXIR OF LIFE

Once, a long, long time ago, there lived a man so terrified of death that he feared living.

The man had unimaginable wealth: He had whole rooms stuffed with jewels, yet their glimmer failed to warm him. He had palaces with views so beautiful that poets wrote songs and artists conjured paintings, yet he never neared their windows, never even stepped foot upon their balconies. Indeed, he never ventured outside, but rather traveled underground, through tunnels, for fear of what lay in wait outside. For fear of *death*.

He owned countless cattle, yet while famine ate through streets where villagers starved, he held sumptuous feasts for his family and privileged guests, feasts that fell sour upon his own stomach, too anxious to digest.

He commanded vast armies skilled in combat and loyal beyond measure, yet their numbers could not make him feel safe.

The world moved by strings tied to his fingertips; anything the man desired, he was granted. He had ships and chariots; servants and sages, all at his disposal.

And the man used them all. He was merciless. He trampled anything in his way, slaughtered any who dared voice dissent, squashed villages—whole provinces—that did not bow to him. The man built giant walls stocked with parapets and soldiers, walls that stretched across the earth and sent tremors through his enemies. No one dared cross such a man as this. And so, they swore allegiance instead.

From mountaintops to seashores, through fields of rice and desert sands, everyone swore their allegiance to this man. He was honored, revered. At a single gesture, his subjects would gladly sacrifice their lives for him.

Yes, this man was all-powerful. In the eyes of those in his shadow (and that was everyone), he was a god.

Yet there was one thing he could not achieve. One thing alone:

He could not defeat death.

The man obsessed over it; death became his every-waking thought: how to trick it, how to avoid it. Nothing was safe. Death lurked around every corner. Every moment of every day was tied to this single idea.

And so, the man who had it all, the man with the greatest wealth and vastest lands, the man with the world's power, the man with everything on earth to live for, feared life itself.

CHAPTER 9

This did not sit well with him.

He controlled everything. He controlled the *world*. If he wished it, it must be so. That was the only way. There *must* be an elixir to defeat death. He knew it must exist; he could *feel* it.

And so, he set scholars to work, hundreds of the world's wisest men, searching scrolls, scouring any record that might give a glimpse, that might prove that such a thing existed. That somewhere there was an elixir of eternal life.

And then, after years of work, when those same scholars had discovered no such thing to report, the man put them all to death.

The scholars had failed him; if he wished it, it must be so. It was the only way.

There *must* be an elixir of eternal life.

Ships sailed, armies marched, more scholars shook in their seats to study ancient documents. Maidens were sacrificed and incense burned at alters, all for the sake of finding an elixir.

Who knows what else was done.

I shudder to think ....

This is the story of the Emperor Qin Shi Huang, the first emperor of China. This man was real. He did all of these things I've said and more.

"But did he find it?"

"What, child?"

"The elixir! The key to eternal life!"

"Oh. Well, some say that he did. In fact, some say that it was I who gave it to him."

"Well, then ... did you?"

"Technically, no."

Silence. So much silence. It crept and throbbed in the vacuum of space. It stretched on and on; it was unbearable, but she knew she must wait. She knew she mustn't interrupt. And then:

"I never gave him an elixir. I gave him the closest thing I knew that could help."

"And that was …?" This came out in a whisper, but the words were clear, compressed, squeezed tight into their spaces.

"Well, that should be obvious, child. I gave him pure energy. Or rather, I told him where he could find it."

Another pause. The Wizard leaned in, his face just inches from Libby's own. She found that she held her breath, his unblinking gaze melting straight into her.

"And now," he said, his voice so very quiet. So quiet, yet it tremored, vibrating its notes through the cave where they sat, almost as if each sound had a tail hooked on its end, flicking colors through the darkness—magenta and green, violet and yellow—tails flashing and swishing through the dark. "May I please see it?"

Libby felt her breath leave her lungs like a balloon deflating. *Whooosh*. Her chest felt heavy, almost painful.

"You-you mean my moonstone necklace?" The question came at a cost. It felt as if she hadn't a drop of air left in her lungs. She took in a great gulp; it was cool and clammy in her mouth, then down it went, into her lungs, but they felt so thin, thin as paper. They couldn't hold anything inside, not even *atoms*.

The whites of the Wizard's eyes gleamed in the dark. He blinked. For that split second, there was nothing to see, nothing at all. Then his eyes fluttered open, and he looked once more into hers. He didn't say a word.

Yes.

He didn't say it, but she could hear his answer. Or perhaps she sensed it, she didn't know.

"But ... I don't have it on me. I had to take it off; it was burning ...."

The Wizard nodded slowly. "Ah, yes. Another Incident, I see. Well, that is to be expected; how could you resist? This place ... it is, shall we say, unique in its construction. But it is there, is it not? It is with you on your journey?"

Libby gulped again, then nodded. *How did he know?* Her head spun; there were so many questions.

"Listen, child. Tomorrow, you will arrive near this place. You will be just outside where we now sit. You will be here, and yet not know that you are. I tell you this so you will understand what to do ...."

"Yes?"

"You must wear the stone. Do not worry. I have made arrangements to stabilize the effect of this place; you will not be harmed ...."

Libby nodded again. Even if she'd wanted, she felt doubtful she could speak. Her throat felt stitched into a straight line. She suddenly found it hard to swallow, even.

"You must wear the stone, and you must follow the path through the tea trees until the plantation ends. Continue on, climbing the slabs of granite steps until you reach a tall boulder the size of a hill. Beside this boulder, you will find a small, spring-fed pool. Now, pay close attention, child. This is the most important part ...."

Libby stared back at the Wizard, so intent on his words she felt paralyzed. She couldn't speak. She couldn't breathe. She couldn't even nod her head. It was as if everything had frozen, even her. Even *time*.

When the Wizard spoke next, the syllables of his words dropped like icicles through the air, clean and sharp. "You must fill your cup with this spring water, then you must drink it. Do not leave anything within the cup. Not even a drop. Then you must destroy it. Do you understand?"

Somehow, Libby found she could once more nod her head. *But what would happen once she did this? And what about Uncle Frank? Ine? The four men?* She could nod her head, but she could not find her voice.

"And another thing, child. The girl who is with you, you must convince her to return home. She is not to be here. You must insist upon it."

But I've tried, thought Libby. *Everyone has tried, and she won't listen. Uncle Frank and me, we don't know what else to do! How are we supposed to convince her of anything when she is so determined? And anyway, she promised she'd go as soon as she meets you. She has helped me so much. Couldn't you allow that? Just give her a second of your time?*

These thoughts and more popped through her head, down to her throat, but still, she couldn't speak them. It was so frustrating.

"And also," she continued, but wait! Was that her voice? Was she suddenly speaking again? This was beyond confusing. "What-what cup?"

The Wizard's eyes lifted, the half-moon whites rising over the dark of his irises. And then, a smile.

"Libby!"

She awoke with a start. Sweat seeped through her clothes, turning them damp and cold against her skin. She shivered, her eyes wide and blinking, adjusting to the darkness.

Uncle Frank sat beside her. "You okay, kiddo?"

"The Wizard!" choked Libby. It had felt so real. How could it have just been a dream? And yet, here she was, camped out on a mountainside with the rest of their expedition ....

"Soon," said Uncle Frank. He spoke softly, careful not to wake Ine and the four men. "Don't worry, kiddo; we'll reach him by tomorrow. Now, go back to sleep. We've got a big day ahead."

Libby gulped in the night air, shivering against its chill, but even so it was a relief to breathe, to feel her lungs fill with air. They ached so. They felt brittle, like the cracked bellows of an ancient accordion. She shivered again and reached for the blanket twisted around her torso. And just then, just as her hand brushed against the cloth, she felt something else, too.

No!

But her fingers reached around, now both hands encircling the object. Libby blinked in disbelief. She glanced up to where Uncle Frank sat in his mobile unit, wondering if he'd noticed, but now, her great uncle's attention was fixed on the stars.

There was no use telling him. He wouldn't understand. *She* didn't understand. But still, it was definitely there. Or rather, it was definitely *here:*

In her hands, she held a tiny, clay cup.

10

THE STOLEN CUP

The next morning arrived with rain, slicking the rocks and softening the earth to mush. The expedition team had eaten their breakfast of steamed buns in silence as they huddled under oil coats, and then they set out once more for the mountaintop.

It was a difficult climb, so when they finally reached the tea trees stretching over the mountainside, Libby nearly sang out in relief. But she didn't, because then she'd have to explain why.

And she hadn't told anyone *why.*

In the light of day, her dream from the night before seemed ridiculous. Unreal. It couldn't possibly have happened.

Yet, in her satchel, she had a new addition to her inventory: A clay cup.

And now here was the tea plantation, just as the Wizard had described.

"I wish to apologize."

Libby turned in surprise to see Ine beside her.

"I know I have been behaving with odd manners," Ine continued without breaking her stride. "I cannot understand why, but I feel that it is necessary to accompany you."

Libby frowned at the path in front of her. This was not going well at all. She had managed to convince Uncle Frank to return her necklace (on the condition she carry it in her satchel and not around her neck), but convincing Ine to return home was another matter altogether. How exactly were they supposed to accomplish that at this point? They couldn't very well send her back on her own, and they couldn't stop their journey just for Ine, either. They were on a *mission*.

"At any rate," resumed Ine, "I was wondering about that stone you have ...."

Libby grimaced. "Yes?"

"May I see it?"

Libby lifted her eyes from the trail to Ine. The girl looked back, her gaze full of questions.

"I don't think that's a very good idea," said Libby.

Ine bit her lower lip, then glanced away.

"But I have been meaning to ask you," added Libby in an attempt to lighten the mood, "how on earth did you get to be so clever? I mean, you're *the smartest* kid I've ever met!"

Ine's expression didn't change. "If your parents were always occupied," she answered flatly, "and if you were moved to a place completely different than anything you had ever known, and if you could not understand anything anyone around you said for the longest time, and if you were the only child within kilometers in your situation, then what is there left to *be* but clever?"

Libby thought about that for a moment. "Moving here … that must have been very hard for you."

Ine shrugged. "I have since made a few friends. I realize I am fortunate to have such a unique experience. Even so, it is not a normal life when books are your main companions. I study them because it helps me not to feel so alone. It gives me a sense of belonging, I suppose you could say."

Libby nodded, thinking once again about *her* book: the Brothers Grimm collection she used to read on lazy Sundays. But that was *before*. Before everything changed. And before the book—along with the secret it contained—burst into particulate matter when Zelna was destroyed ….

A breeze rustled through the tea trees, the sound murmuring over the mountainside like an invisible wave, sweeping away her reverie.

"I think I understand," she replied, readjusting the satchel hanging from her waist. "I mean, I know what it's like to feel alone; to feel like no one gets you. Before Ginny came along, I didn't have any friends. Everyone thought I was a weirdo."

"Weirdo?"

"Oh!" Libby laughed. "It means to be different. Like, people don't want to be around you because you make them uncomfortable."

They continued walking through the plantation, both of them falling into silence. When they reached the top of a slope, Libby could see over the shrubby tree tops that carpeted the mountainside in green, their shiny leaves rich with rain. It was beautiful, enchanted even. So much about this place felt that way.

"You do not make me feel uncomfortable," said Ine, peeking up at Libby. "In some ways, I feel as if we have already met before. There is something ... familiar ... about you."

Libby grinned. She was really beginning to like this kid. "Well, I have to admit I've been a little nervous you'll bite me again," she replied teasingly, "but other than that—"

"*Bite* you?" Ine stopped dead in her tracks. "Why on earth would I *bite* you?"

For a second, Libby froze in her steps as well. She looked from Ine to the four men behind her, not knowing what to say. Then she examined her hand once again, where the little tooth marks remained conspicuously missing. In fact, she really was wondering if she *had* imagined the whole thing ....

"Sorry; bad joke, I guess," she blurted, feeling her face grow hot. She tried to laugh it off. "See what I mean? I'm a weirdo."

Ine scowled and resumed her pace through the tea trees. A good thing, too, because Libby needed time to think. Her mind raced over the events since they'd landed in China. What was happening to her? How could it be that something so certain as a bite mark could mysteriously disappear? And here was the other thing: Was she certain she had received it in the first place? Ine acted as if she had no recollection of the incident. So how could she *know?* Wasn't that the real question? Or even more confusing: could it be that the bite marks happened, and also didn't happen? Could there be two entirely different realities existing at the same time? Was that possible?

It felt as if her brain was swelling by the second with questions pushing against her skull—hundreds and hundreds of them—, and the only thing keeping it from exploding was the knowledge that soon she would meet the Wizard ....

The expedition party continued on. Ine in front, then Libby, then the four men carrying Uncle Frank. Occasionally, the four men would pause for a short break, exchanging words in their language that Libby could not understand, but otherwise the mountainside was silent, with only the breeze rustling through the tea trees from time to time.

And then, after what felt like hours, the plantation stopped and before them spread a path with stone slabs leading up, up, up.

"The granite steps," Libby whispered.

Ine glanced sharply at her. "Do you know this place?"

"N-no. I just ... well, it looks like granite steps, right?"

Ine regarded her with those wide, solemn eyes but said nothing more. Libby's heart fluttered. Soon. Very, very soon. It was hard to believe. After so long; after such an unlikely journey, to finally be here. It was another one of those instances:

It seemed impossible.

They began to climb.

The rocks were wide and flat, wide enough for the four men to carry Uncle Frank on his platform. The granite steps arched over the mountainside like the spine of a giant dragon.

After six minutes of climbing, Libby could see the precipice up ahead, where the stones evened out. Just the sight of it sent her heart jittering, practically rattling her ribs. She was electrified with expectation. Terrified, too. *What now? What next? What about Uncle Frank?*

She didn't know. And she couldn't tell him. She dared not even *look* at him. It was the first time in her life that she'd kept such a secret.

She reached level ground, her legs quivering with each step, her forehead and the back of her neck beading with sweat, turning cold and clammy in the air. Ahead, not fifty feet from where she stood, she saw a tall boulder. A tall boulder the size of a hill. And beside that boulder, she saw a small, spring-fed pool.

The jittering in her heart shot tremors through her limbs. With each step, her knees dissolved into gelatin, her feet into awkward, flapping paddles that stumbled over the ground. Her sight swam dizzily so that the boulder and the little pool blurred together in her vision. *What was happening?* She didn't know. She suddenly felt panicked. She should tell Uncle Frank, but she knew that she couldn't. If she told him what the Wizard had instructed her to do, he wouldn't allow it. There was no way he'd let her do something without him by her side, much less do something before he'd tested it first ….

But if they were to find a way to return home, if they were

to somehow get back to their own time, to return to her parents, if they had any hope at all for their lives back, then she *had* to follow the Wizard's instructions.

She stumbled toward the little pool, her pace quickening, her hands fumbling at the embroidered satchel hanging from her belt. And even as Libby moved faster and faster toward that pool, Ine somehow remained exactly by her side, watching her every step as if the girl were a wild animal stalking its prey, never falling behind, never breaking eye contact.

It was uncanny.

Libby gulped in deep breaths of air. Her hand slipped into the satchel and found purchase on the moonstone. She pulled it out. Brilliant blue dazzled everywhere.

"Libby, what are you doing?"

She dared not look at Uncle Frank. If she did, she'd change her mind. She'd chicken out. She'd tell him everything ….

She slipped the chain of her moonstone over her neck, trying to ignore the blazing blue, trying to ignore Ine's scrutiny. Next, she grabbed the little cup from her satchel.

"Kiddo, whatever you're doing, please wait! Let's take a bit of a rest, okay?" Uncle Frank's voice cut through the mountain air, sharp with worry.

He knew.

If anyone could understand Libby by a single glance, it was her Uncle Frank.

"Please, Libby!"

She still didn't turn. But she couldn't help but catch Ine's gaze because the girl stepped closer, now not even a foot away.

Ine didn't say anything. She didn't need to. Those haunted eyes just *stuck* to her like an invisible force.

And then, just as Libby pulled out the little cup, she heard the sound of pounding hooves. *How very strange.*

"Ine! Ine, *mein Liebling!*"

At this, Libby turned. And to her astonishment, just behind the four men carrying an extremely agitated Uncle Frank, galloped a woman with wild, blonde hair.

"*Mama!*" Ine's voice was barely a whisper, but her face filled with emotion—emotion Libby had never seen register there before. Happiness. Surprise. Confusion. Perhaps shame? Libby wasn't sure, but then that familiar resolute expression settled back into Ine's eyes.

"Whatever it is you are doing," she murmured to Libby, "you had better hurry."

Libby glanced from Ine to the cup in her hands to the galloping woman who was now passing Uncle Frank and his entourage. Behind Uncle Frank, she saw two more horses with their riders appear from the steps, and she looked from them back to Uncle Frank.

His gaze was locked on her. It had never left. "I don't know what you are planning, kiddo," he said, and he was close enough now that he needn't call out; he was right there, perhaps ten feet away, but the heaviness in his voice remained, the *dread*, "but wait for me. Let's talk this through."

The blonde woman came to a stop. She towered above them both, then flicked off her saddle, agile as a whip. At the same time, Ine hissed:

"Hurry!"

Libby turned once more to Uncle Frank, her heart twisting in her chest. More than anything, she wanted to run to him, to throw her arms around his neck, to ask him what she should do.

"I love you," she said instead, but her throat contracted so she could barely get it out.

"No, Libby!"

She dipped the cup in the pool and drank. At the same time, the woman reached down, her arms stretching toward her daughter, relief and adoration blazing across her face. The water slipped down Libby's throat, icy cold. She raised her hand to smash the cup against the boulder ....

A push.

She stumbled. Quick as lightning, Ine snatched the cup from her hand.

The blonde woman's arms wrapped around her daughter, heaving sobs, laughing and scolding and fussing and kissing. The girl was *loved*.

It was all happening so fast. Uncle Frank's face, nothing but pure horror. Ine's eyes, never leaving Libby, even with her mother there. Even as the little girl rocked in her mother's tearful embrace, she tilted that stolen cup to her lips, shaking out a single, last drop ....

The water froze in Libby's chest, expanding by the second. She couldn't breathe. Her lungs stretched flat. It was like her dream.

And then ...

Nothing.

11

THE WIZARD'S CAVE

I t was so dark.

Libby realized a hand clung onto her own, small fingers digging into her palm like metal hooks. *Ine.*

Deep breath.

"Where are we?" Ine's voice trembled in the darkness.

"Th-the Wizard's cave, I think," whispered Libby. She closed her eyes, then opened them again while forcing herself to breathe: In through her nose, out through her mouth. In, then out. Don't panic.

It was so, so dark.

A cough, a scuffling sound and then ….

"Goodness sakes! What kind of an entrance is this? And after all that preparation!"

"He-hello?" Libby's voice shook into the void. "C-can you hear me?"

The sizzle of a match. Libby saw a brass lantern held high in the air, and now she could see part of a man's face.

"Of course I can *hear* you!" replied the man, though she could only see his eyes and forehead. "What a silly question!"

"Are you——" she pressed on, forcing herself to speak, willing her throat to function, but everything on her shook so forcibly that it was a wonder she could stand, much less talk, "are you the Wizard?"

Through the glow of the lantern, the man's eyes grew large. "Honestly, child, I shall not even dignify that with an answer! And who, may I ask, are *you?*"

Libby swallowed hard. Her throat felt like it had glued itself together. "I-I'm Libby," she managed in a gasp. "Liberty Frye."

"Hmm," said the man.

"We … er, met last night?

The glowing eyes narrowed, then darted to her side. "Then, who is *that?*"

Libby felt her hand squeezed tighter. She tore her gaze from the Wizard to where her friend stood. In the weak light, she could barely make out Ine's face, but she could see that the little girl's eyes were flung wide open.

"This," Libby began, but she had to stop and swallow again. "This is Ine. She … um, she sort of tagged along by accident."

"Indeed." The Wizard's eyes rose up and up, like they had in her dream, showing whites rising from the lower lids.

"Sorry," she added hastily.

Silence.

"Yes," the Wizard sighed after a moment. "As am I."

More silence. Libby glared down at Ine, expecting her to say *something* by way of explanation, but the little girl remained frozen at her side, her fingers a veritable vise on her hand.

The Wizard shuffled over the ground, his lantern illuminating the few inches around him. "These blasted birds!" he fussed, the lantern light wobbling through the darkness. "Each time I think I have the matter solved, they go and—there!"

Light flooded the cave, blinding Libby with the sudden radiance. And then, when her eyes focused, she saw that they weren't in a cave at all. They were in …

"A palace?" She exhaled, her eyes rolling from the towering white walls to the curved, ornate molding to the domed, golden ceiling far above. "How … I mean, what … or rather—"

"Cogent speech!" interjected the Wizard, whom Libby now saw was adjusting his bowtie in a bespangled mirror. "Pithy observations! Succinct questions! All are welcome here, child, but I do detest all this stuttering and beating about the bush! What *is it* that you mean to ask?"

Libby blinked hard. Lining the sides of the room in which they stood, golden phoenixes perched upon sconces jutting from the walls. One by one, a phoenix would burst into flames, roaring bright as its form disintegrated to ash, then surged together once more at its base, a shimmering swirl of glittering ashes that somehow formed into a phoenix again! Their spontaneous combustions were synced in such a way that, all around the room, the number of phoenixes exploding into fire was perfectly coordinated with those regenerating so that the exploding birds, by all appearances, provided the sole light source.

"But I thought …," Libby tried again—it was extremely difficult to form a thought with exploding birds all around— and just then one near her head burst into flames. "Aghh!"

"WHAT?"

She scrambled away from the wall, dragging a clinging Ine along with her. "I thought you lived in a cave!"

In her mind, this had seemed like a sensible starting point. Much to Libby's dismay, however, the Wizard obviously disagreed.

"Now, why," he retorted, pivoting from his mirror so that he faced her, "would a *wizard* choose to live in a cave? Is that really what you think of me? That, after thousands of years of wizarding, all I can come up with is an earthen hovel?"

Libby peeped down at Ine, who looked back at her.

"He has a point," whispered Ine.

"And I know what you're thinking," continued the Wizard, whose appearance Libby was starting to take in, and the truth of it was he looked nothing like she'd imagined.

Libby gawked, too stunned to realize how rude she was being (or that her hand was developing a serious cramp from Ine's grip) because all she could think of at that moment was how young the Wizard looked. Shouldn't he be older? He'd just said himself that he'd been wizarding for *thousands* of years!

But his skin remained remarkably smooth and his hair jet black, cropped to chin length and slicked back in a rather jaunty fashion. Were wizards normally jaunty? She hadn't thought so; she'd always imaged wizards with long, flowing beards wearing robes and pointy hats!

Libby continued staring, now taking in the rest of the Wizard's decidedly unwizardly appearance. He was slim and fit, of average height, and he sported a goatee and a mustache that was groomed to a medium width and curled up slightly at the edges, neatly waxed. He wore tailored slacks (dark grey), a crisp white button-down shirt complete with a bowtie (canary yellow with small polka dots) and dark suspenders. In fact, Libby realized as she regarded him with wonder, he looked much more like an old-fashioned movie star than a wizard, and the only thing that reminded her that she hadn't suddenly been transported to a movie set was the fact that the Wizard wore no socks or shoes.

Libby gaped at the Wizard's bare feet, which were a bit of a shock to witness. It just didn't fit with the rest of his formal attire, but then she realized he was examining her boots with equal amazement.

"Remarkable!" he murmured as if to himself. "You've simply enormous feet! But that's off topic, and really what can be done? Back to what you're thinking …."

Libby fidgeted.

"You're thinking," he continued, completely oblivious to Libby's befuddlement, "that I have made a grave error. And now you question my judgment upon everything, don't you?"

Libby averted her gaze as she considered his question. Did she? She'd no idea. Maybe. This was, after all, a very strange way to meet a person, but then again, she'd never met a wizard before ….

"I see you struggle with conversational skills," he continued with obvious impatience. "Nonetheless, opening and closing your mouth like a blowfish is not an acceptable substitute for words!"

"Sorry," she managed to reply. She absently flexed her left hand, realizing Ine had finally released her hold. "It must be all the, er, *transporting* that just took place. I feel a little out of sorts, I guess. And I-I am not sure what you mean by your judgment?"

The Wizard's eyebrows rose to new heights. "This dimension, child!" he cried in exasperation. "I assume you find it quite rude! As if it isn't enough to find yourself in China, circa 1871. That is where we are, after all, is it not? Or at least *you* are …."

Libby was pretty sure she nodded.

"After all," the Wizard said, plucking a piece of chalk from his lapel and turning to the bespangled mirror, "I gave you absolutely no preparation whatsoever! Now." He pulled the chalk across the surface of what had—just moments before—been the mirror, but now, inexplicably, had transformed into a chalkboard. "What do you see?"

Libby squinted at the chalkboard, too confounded to ask how he'd just *done* that. She concentrated on his drawing, thinking it best to just go along. "A … straight line?"

"Exactly! But do you see anything *less?* Anything *more?* Something this might be *a part of?*"

"Um, no?"

The Wizard turned and scratched across the chalkboard again. "And now?"

Libby examined the board, feeling so perplexed by this bizarre person that it was really quite difficult to concentrate.... "Now I see a square."

The Wizard nodded, then turned to the chalkboard once more. "And now?"

"It's ... it's a cube," said Libby. "Like a box."

"And now?" asked the Wizard, drawing, impossibly, trees and houses beside the cube so it looked as if the cube were moving past them and, as it did so, changing the whole picture from a scene of a morning into that of evening ....

"Now it seems like ...," struggled Libby, because at this point her head was killing her, and she wasn't sure if it was from the strange journey she'd just experienced or from simply trying to keep up with the Wizard, "it seems like it's showing the cube moving down a street or something from morning into the night ...."

"Yes!" cried the Wizard, which made Libby accidentally stumble against a phoenix, but thankfully she had the foresight to jump away before it singed her eyebrows. "So you see, this illustrates what you currently understand as our four dimensions, to wit: length, width, depth ... and time! Or to put it another way, these four dimensions weave together to create what you know as space-time."

Libby studied the chalkboard. She was just about to ask more about the space-time part when the Wizard continued.

"Now, what if I were to tell you that *even more* dimensions exist; many more, but you simply don't perceive them because your mind is not able to *imagine* them yet? Just as, before I turned the one-dimensional line into the two-dimensional square into a three-dimensional cube into four-dimensional *space-time*, you only perceived a line!"

Libby looked to the walls where the phoenixes continued to spontaneously combust, racking her brain for a suitable reply, but she had absolutely no idea how to respond.

The Wizard threw up his hands, sending the chalk flinging across the room.

"So," blurted Libby, terrified he was about to lose his temper, and the one thing she was certain of at this particular juncture was that a Wizard in a foul temper was probably a situation best avoided, "are you saying that we're in another dimension—like a fifth or sixth or seventh dimension or something—but I don't see it because my mind doesn't understand what it is?"

"Mensch Meier!" murmured Ine under her breath.

"Precisely!" The Wizard beamed, then he spun on his heel and grabbed a tray that rested on a table between two birds currently disintegrating into ash. "Come!" he called, now carrying the tray as he padded toward a hallway. "After all the traveling you've done, you must be absolutely famished!"

Libby followed the Wizard, growing more bewildered with each step, and not just because of the phoenixes or the lecture on dimensions or even the Wizard's bare feet. Because she was sure that, when the lights first came on, the only thing surrounding them had been the huge, white room with the golden ceiling and exploding birds. But now they were passing through a cavernous hallway that was so big it could swallow her family's entire house. How could she not have noticed it until just now? And yet she was sure it hadn't been there ... it couldn't have just *appeared,* could it?

"Have a seat!" commanded the Wizard, and much to Libby's astonishment, she found they were no longer in a hallway, but rather in the middle of an enormous library, complete with leather armchairs, polished maple side tables, a fire crackling in a marble fireplace and a large oil painting perched over the mantle. All around, shelves stuffed with books lined the room and even stretched above them for two more stories.

"How did you *do* that?" she gasped.

"What you need," the Wizard said, "is a good cup of tea!"

And before Libby could consider whether she was thirsty or not, she felt something bump into the back of her legs, knocking her off balance so that she fell backward. Except she didn't fall, because the thing that had knocked into her was a squishy leather chair that just happened to scoop her up so she found herself sitting. And in her hand, which she'd raised to catch her balance, she now held a cup and saucer. Libby's eyes twitched.

"It is rude," declared the Wizard, "to decline hospitality. Now are you going to drink your tea or just sit there and goggle at it?"

Libby decided she'd better drink it, so she lifted the cup to her lips, her shaking hands sending waves through the amber liquid. She had no idea what she was about to drink; it could be tea, it could be poison, it could be another magical elixir that would send her back to Uncle Frank. She didn't know and was too baffled to ask. So she drank, and when she lowered the cup back to its saucer, she saw that they remained in the library, with all three of them sitting in armchairs with their respective cups of tea.

Except there was one thing about the room that was decidedly different ....

Libby's gaze arched from Ine and the Wizard to the cheery, crackling fire. And then her eyes lifted up, up, up, until they met the oil painting perched on the mantel overhead.

"Oh!" she said, nearly spilling her tea all over her lap. She fixated on the painting, barely believing her eyes, but no, no, no, she was absolutely sure:

That oil painting had quite mysteriously ... well, it had begun to *swirl*.

12

A Very Peculiar Tea Party

I t wasn't just a *swirl,* it was more like a hurricane: churning and spinning, faster and faster. And it had a sound to it, like a distant, high-pitched howl.

"Good tea, no?"

Libby turned from the swirling painting to see the Wizard beaming at her. She cleared her throat, then turned once more to the painting, only now the swirling colors appeared to be moving *out* from the gilded frame so that the hurricane of blues and greens and yellows projected into the room, growing wider by the minute.

"What *is* that?" she whispered, and her heart thumped and bumped inside her as she turned to Ine.

But Ine didn't reply. The girl sat as if frozen inside the large armchair, her sight locked on the swirling colors, her teacup tipped in one hand so the remaining liquid trembled precariously at the rim.

"That," replied the Wizard, "is many things, child, but you've already observed that it is a painting."

"But … it's moving!"

The Wizard smiled and took another sip of tea. "Everything in the universe is moving. Didn't you know? We're all just a collection of bouncing, zipping, zapping particles! And if we look even closer … well, then we might not see anything at all!"

Libby blinked at the Wizard. None of this made a lick of sense, and the one thing she needed above all else at the moment was to make sense of *something*. She forced her attention from the violent swirl.

"Earlier," she began, grappling at the random thoughts jumping about in her brain, "you said something … er, strange …."

"Well, I certainly hope so! What's the point otherwise?"

"I mean, you said that *I* am in China, circa 1871 …."

"Aren't you?"

"Well, yes," bumbled Libby, feeling increasingly disoriented by this odd man, "but what I mean is, you made it a point to talk about where—and when—we are, but then you said 'at least you are,' as if to imply that I am in 1871 China …"

"Yes?"

"… but you aren't!"

The Wizard tilted his head so it rested at the back of his chair, his eyes angled down as he considered her.

"Thank goodness," he murmured.

Libby squeezed her eyes shut and shook her head again, as if she could rattle whatever sense she had left into place. "Sorry? I don't understand …."

"I only mean I am relieved to see evidence of that intellect I was so sure you possessed. Up until now, you have acted more or less like a startled guppy …. I don't know why I keep comparing you to fish, but there you have it …." He paused to take another sip of tea as he regarded her. "But I see now that your analytical functions have kicked in. It's about time because we have so much to discuss!"

Well, Libby had to agree with that. There was indeed *so much* to discuss, and she was just about to delve into things when she cried out instead, because the library and the cozy fire suddenly vanished, and in their place she found that she and Ine and the Wizard remained seated in their leather chairs … with absolutely nothing around them at all. No room, no walls, no ceiling, no floor ….

"I see your consternation," said the Wizard, who had somehow made his teacup disappear as they hovered in empty space. "But the explanation is really quite simple, child. I hope you have observed that your friend appears to be remarkably unresponsive?"

Libby glanced at Ine, who remained seated as she had before, her teacup still tilted in the exact same position. "Is she okay?"

"She's fine," assured the Wizard. "As are you, child. Or as fine as is possible, I should amend. And even though you perceive that we are floating in a complete abyss, we are as snug and comfortable as we had been in the library, do you disagree?"

It was all Libby could do to breathe, much less argue, so she settled on shaking her head.

"And yet, despite these facts, your sense of alarm has increased a hundredfold. What I mean to say is, you are just as safe—or unsafe—as you had been in the library, but suddenly you feel decidedly less secure. Am I wrong?"

Libby shook her head again, then realized that the sound jingling in her ears was her own teacup and saucer rattling together in her hands. Carefully, she placed them on a table that suddenly floated beside her. The Wizard smiled again.

"You see? It is all a matter of perception. Oh, I could wax on and on about it. What is reality? Life? Love? What is the perfect ratio of yak cheese to wine? Important questions, all, yet utterly pointless!"

A sparrow flew by, then fluttered to a stop on the Wizard's head.

"I merely say this to lend illustration," continued the Wizard, "of our propensity to squash and categorize things in ridiculous ways because their true essence is so vast—or perhaps actually so *simple*—that we cannot comprehend them. So we make up stories to fit them into what is already familiar and ignore things we should be paying attention to. Just as your mind currently perceives that we are floating in the sky and ignores the fact that we are also still in the library. Or mostly. Don't you agree?"

Libby wasn't sure if she did or if she didn't. In fact, she wasn't entirely sure what the Wizard was talking about. The only thing she knew for certain at the moment was that a sparrow was making a nest on his head ....

"So, you're saying," she grappled, "that all of this is simply perception and not what's actually real? Is that it?"

The Wizard lowered his eyes, an amused smile tugging at his lips.

"Very good, child. You are living up to your reputation after all; I am utterly relieved to find you in working order! But to address your previous question: Yes!"

"Yes?"

"Yes. Yes, you are in China, circa 1871. Yes, that's where your mind and body are perceiving the present, at least. Yes, I am not necessarily in that same state. Yes, none of this is real and yes, all of this *is* real. Try to imagine it, Liberty Frye:

"Everything we perceive as solid ... or full ... or empty ... or even existing in the *present* ... all of it is a collection of holes and wrinkles and gaps, even time. And if we can find ways to wiggle into those gaps, we may *perceive* that our reality has changed, when in fact, we are still sitting in the library, but we've wiggled ourselves into a gap within that library."

Libby stared at her hands.

The Wizard sighed. "If it helps, think of it like a dream. Just as you and I met last night—when I gave you *explicit* instructions that you promptly disregarded—," he paused to throw a sour look Ine's way, "so we are meeting once again! You see? You were able to meet with me, while all that evening, you also remained snug at your campsite with your Uncle Frank by your side."

"But … but that doesn't make any sense! I wasn't *dreaming* when I saw the boulder and the pool, just as you'd described! Or when I drank from that little cup! I am sure of it!"

"But when you dreamed you first met me," replied the Wizard with a sly grin, "didn't that seem just as real?"

Libby twisted her fingers together, then peered over to the side table suspended in the air beside her.

"Perception!" concluded the Wizard. "Now, on to Phase Two!"

And just then, Ine dropped her teacup and squirmed inside her chair, instantly alert once more. Where the teacup went, Libby had no idea, but as she followed Ine's gaze, she saw that they were once again in the library. Everything was just as it had been before, except the swirling mass of color had stopped moving through the room and now stood in front of them, the size of a front door. And the colors were no longer discernable but rather a blur of silvery-grey, spinning so fast and liquid that it actually appeared to stand still.

13

THE PORTAL TO NOWHERE

Ine stared at her hands. "What happened to my tea?"

"You were done with it, my dear," replied the Wizard. Then he began nibbling on a piece of toast, completely disinterested that a sparrow was weaving bits of his hair into its nest. "Now, we must unfortunately cut to the chase," he declared through his munching. "We haven't all day; even my methods touch into your conventions of time, and there is only so long I can keep you both outside on the ground with your loved ones mooning over you like grief-struck orangutans."

Libby looked to Ine, who looked back at Libby, her eyes as wide as windows.

"I … beg your pardon?" Ine said.

The Wizard dipped the corner of his toast into a soft-boiled egg that hovered before him. "It is what I was trying to explain to your friend earlier," he replied after a moment, dabbing at his mouth with a napkin. "Our perceptions can really get in the way of things, which is why I did you the courtesy of a momentary lapse of consciousness." He paused to smile benevolently at Ine. "But I am afraid to say you have brought this on yourself, my dear. Curiosity killed the cat, so to speak, but since you are not a cat, something much more interesting is going to happen. And the least I can do for you is to arm you with certain bits of information."

Ine swallowed.

"First, I should explain that, even as we sit here enjoying each other's company," he continued as the two girls gawked at each other in bewilderment, "your physical bodies remain outside where you last left them … for now. That is to say, your mother and your great uncle," the Wizard nodded in turn to each of them, "are presently fretting their heads off over your unconscious forms. Now, it was only supposed to be *one* of you. The other came … uninvited." He paused again to glance meaningfully at Ine, who at this point looked so alarmed Libby was afraid she'd forgotten to breathe.

"Secondly," continued the Wizard, "you should know that while we've spent a good fifteen minutes in this glorious place, to your loved ones, you've only been unconscious for a minute at most."

"You mean …," blurted Libby, "we're here but we're also still outside? Like, Uncle Frank is with me at this exact moment?"

"Exactly."

"But that's …."

"Impossible?" smiled the Wizard. "I know you're clever enough to have learned something about the word *impossible*. What is 'impossible' really, except magic? And what is magic? Well, an excellent writer a few decades from now best sums it up! He said … or rather *will* say …," the Wizard stopped to chuckle at this, "forgive me, I realize my humor might be confusing to you; at any rate, this author will one day declare: 'Magic is just science that we don't understand yet.'" The Wizard leaned his head back, his expression suddenly far, far away. "That's Artie for you," he chuckled again, his voice soft with nostalgia. "We did have some lovely chats …."

Libby shook her head. The swirling, silvery-grey doorway remained in front of her, and suddenly she felt afraid of it.

"At any rate, you do know a thing or two about magic. And of time. You've experienced yourself the sensation of stepping through moments, have you not?" The Wizard leaned toward her. "That, while things appear to move at a certain speed to everyone else, to you they slow down? Now, how would you explain *that?*"

Libby twisted her hands, thinking over the Wizard's words. Did he know? Had he somehow seen her two months ago, when she'd been able to slow down rocks being thrown at their ship? Or the bullets, even, when Kai and the prisoners overthrew those awful pirates? Had he seen what she could do … something she couldn't understand herself? Both those moments were exactly as the Wizard had just described: while time had passed in the same way for others, sometimes, somehow, she'd found a way to step *between* it ....

Were those the gaps the Wizard had just been talking about? Gaps in time? They must be.

Libby glimpsed at her twisting hands, absently wondering once more what had happened to those bite marks.

"Ah," said the Wizard, following her gaze. "*That* goes back to what we were discussing earlier, about our perceptions. Can we ever really know what is real? What has or has not happened? If you don't know of a certain event that is occurring halfway around the world, for example, does it make it any less true? And yet, in your mind, that same event does not exist, because you don't know of it. So which is correct? Which reality is authentic?"

Libby stared harder at her hands, wishing she could use them to still the swimming of her thoughts.

"Which leads me to my third point," continued the Wizard, who didn't seem to share Libby's bewilderment in the least. "It is one thing to learn how to *perceive* and *work between* time, as we've just been discussing, and another thing to *bend* it." He glanced from Libby to Ine, and that familiar grin that had flickered playfully across his face now curved into a frown.

"Now *that*," continued the Wizard, once again studying Libby so intently that her skin prickled in response, as if that alert, watchful gaze was somehow seeping into her ..., "that takes *energy.*"

Fear gripped Libby's gut, and for reasons she didn't quite understand, she felt a terrible urge to protect Ine against this

Wizard, to send her away from this place where things and words made no sense ....

"I'll give you a hint," he resumed, his cadence picking up. "What you have been referring to as *powers*—you know, all that witch stuff that has so occupied your mind of late—it is really all just a matter of energy combined with perception. We've already talked some about *perception*. As for energy ...," he leaned in, rubbing his hands as if warming them over a fire, "oh, Liberty Frye, how *much* of it you have!"

Libby's skin rippled at his words, goose bumps rising like tiny volcanoes over her body. The Wizard leaned closer.

"Think of your recent birthday," he almost whispered, "when your energy just happened to tangle with that of the moonstone at the exact moment your great uncle's invention was activated. That is when you first bent time. I confess I have waited a long while for that phenomenon. But who else has their own binary star system—a reservoir of negative energy so immense it can create its own gravitational field?"

"Grav-gravitational field?" repeated Libby.

The Wizard nodded. "But of course. Did Sabine not share that bit of information with you, all those months ago when she first told you of your powers?"

"Sabine?" whispered Ine.

"It is like an enormous magnet, this binary star system of yours," he continued, oblivious to Ine's question. "And it sucks more and more energy as you grow; you can't even help it. You probably don't even know that you're doing it!"

"I don't!"

"But you *must* have guessed by now," the Wizard continued, "that your source has grown even greater since the demise of the individual you know as Zelna? The gravity you command has grown so powerful, it can suck energy from anything it comes in contact with. Consider that moonstone around your neck, for instance. Was it not through you that it collected itself as one again? Who else could command such power? There is *nothing* like you on earth!"

Libby stared at the Wizard. "So ... so you're saying," she began, struggling to digest the meaning behind his words, "... you're saying Zelna is completely gone? That all those *incidents* that have happened to me are just ...," she stopped, too overwhelmed to finish.

The Wizard closed his eyes as he leaned back in his chair. "Nothing that exists is ever gone, it just changes form. And what was once *her* energy ... is now almost entirely *yours*."

Libby took another deep breath, her mind racing faster and faster, and each answer the Wizard gave only spawned more questions in its place.

"You saw her explode into particles of matter, did you not?" continued the Wizard as if sensing her struggle. "But even then, even in such a *moment of crisis,* I imagine the part of you that craves such energy couldn't help but take some, just a bit to feed the beast, so to speak. You may have fought it; I can only assume you did. But later, that part of you grew hungry once more, too hungry to keep down, pulling what was left of her energy into you. You have quite an appetite, Liberty Frye."

Libby sat in her chair, momentarily speechless, the Wizard's words ringing in her ears. With each second, they untangled themselves in her mind, their meaning sinking in. She remembered that anxious expression in Uncle Frank's eyes the other night on the ship, that look of fear … not just fear *for* her, but … fear *of* her. That's what it was.

Libby suddenly felt as if she might throw up.

"It's—it's *me!*"

The Wizard raised an eyebrow. "What is, child?"

Libby focused on the portal swirling before them, as if it could somehow clarify her thoughts.

"You just told me that I … I *suck* energy; that these *incidents* I have are really just me … gathering energy from other sources, like the energy that once belonged to Zelna, right?"

The Wizard looked interested. "Go on."

"Then …," Libby gulped, forcing the bile back down her throat, "then it's me. *I'm* the one making my mother sick. It's true, isn't it? I'm … I'm trying to take her energy; I'm doing it without even knowing! And all along I thought it was still Zelna!"

The Wizard remained resting against his chair, but now his eyes lifted up, locking on hers, holding them fast with his gaze. "I would guess you have quite a battle raging inside that mind of yours," he replied quietly. "Perhaps the moonstone magnifies this hunger. Perhaps the part of you that craves *more* simply takes over from time to time; it fights against you; against your mind. Which part will eventually win? Will it be your strength or your weakness? Only time will tell, Liberty Frye."

And the sound of that pronouncement unleashed all of Libby's fears. She turned to Ine, grabbing her by the arm. "Go back!" she whispered. "If you can, if there is any way you know how, please go back!"

Ine's eyes flicked up, her gaze meeting Libby's, and it was like that moment on the ship, when it felt to Libby as if she were staring into mirrors ….

The Wizard sighed. "Is that not why you are here, child? To go back? I do hope so because I have such wonderful plans!" And his dark eyes grew bright, bright as stars in a clear night sky. "Do you recall your dream from the night before?" he continued, his voice soft, almost trembling with eagerness. "About the emperor? Well, very, very soon, you shall be visiting his tomb, and that nifty moonstone about your neck will change … well, it will change *everything.*"

Both girls turned from each other to the Wizard.

"Now, Ine, my dear," said the Wizard, straightening in his chair as he brushed crumbs from his shirt. "Do you mind showing me that little souvenir you snitched from your friend's satchel?"

Ine gaped at him, her face draining to white. Slowly, she turned to Libby. "I … I just wanted a closer look," she whispered. "I planned to return it …."

She reached into her cape pocket.

"Hello, Barvultmir," smiled the Wizard, just as Ine produced a dried purple berry in the palm of her hand. She opened her mouth as if to speak, but instead a howling wind picked up, whipping around them, drowning out all sound.

And within that roaring void, a beam of hot, white light burst from Libby's moonstone, latching to the swirling portal before them, twisting the portal faster and faster.

The dread Libby had felt before seemed to explode out of her; she lunged toward Ine, desperate to protect her, her fingers splayed to grab at Ine's arm, her hand, her hair, anything at all. But that swirling doorway lurched forward, sharper than wind, more precise than lightning and much, much faster than Libby. It lurched forward like open jaws, howling so fiercely that Libby trembled and howled, too, reaching for her friend as the doorway swallowed Ine, nothing but blackness and wind and those terrible howls. It took less than a single second, all of it.

"And now," said the Wizard, "please take your walkie-talkie out of your bag, child. I believe we have a call to make."

14

ᴄʜᴇ ᴠᴀɴɪsʜɪɴɢ

"Phase Three."

A thousand things were happening, but to Uncle Frank and Ine's mother, they saw only one. And even as the Wizard pronounced those words; even as they left his mouth in a dimension they could not see but was as close and as real as the boulder by which they stooped, nothing mattered, nothing existed but the girl they each held in their arms.

Liesel Herrmann wept, her arms stretched over her precious daughter who lay still and white on the ground. As for Uncle Frank, the tears were there, but terror had frozen them inside. He blinked in disbelief as he cradled Libby in his lap, his back to the boulder and his legs stretched feebly over the ground.

"Libby, kiddo, wake up, please wake up," he whispered, his gaze flicking from Libby's cold brow to the broken clay cup in Ine's hand.

And then, from under his fingertips, he felt a sudden change:

The brow of his grandniece grew warmer and then, in a matter of seconds, warmer and warmer and warmer until her forehead practically boiled with heat and the vessels at her temple throbbed like tangles of swollen garden hose. "What?" He caught his breath, glancing to Liesel to see if she, too, noticed such a change.

Liesel Herrmann lifted her head from her daughter's chest. "There is a warmth …" she whispered.

"Water," said Uncle Frank, gesturing to the pool beside Liesel, then he fumbled at the cloth tied around Libby's head. "Please, could you help? Dip this in the pool for her. She needs to cool down. She … NO!"

The sound left his lips as a shriek, and for that split second, Liesel could only blink back at him in astonishment. But then, ever so slowly, she followed his gaze to Libby.

She gasped. Her blue eyes filled with horror. And in that moment, you could see the struggle: the instinct to turn to her own child, to see if the same had happened to her, and yet the dread of doing so, the dread of seeing the *truth*. But she did.

And sometimes, the flick of an eye can feel like a lifetime.

Ine's mother gaped down at the spot where her daughter had lain in her arms. No gasp left her lips this time, no words, no sounds. Liesel Herrmann was without breath or thought.

"They're gone." Uncle Frank's voice came out as a moan, broken and shattered as his spine. "They're GONE!"

Liesel continued to stare at the spot where, seconds before, her daughter had been.

The tea plantation remained glistening under the sky. The flat, granite steps leading to this place still arched over the ground. The sun slipped lower in the sky as expected, the boulder and pool stood still and serene. Liesel Herrmann's two companions turned from where they stood by the pool, their eyes sharp with shock.

Because Ine was gone. Disappeared.

And Libby was gone.

Where, seconds before, two girls had appeared to sleep on the ground, there only remained earth. And stone.

Down the mountainside and over the river valley, the *Liberté* waded near the willow trees. And on its deck, facing upriver, Ginny and Sal stood, speechless.

"Are you *listening*, Ginny?" came Libby's tearful voice from the walkie-talkie's speaker.

"Y-yes," Ginny finally stammered. She held her walkie-talkie tight in both hands, clutching it so fiercely that, had she not been so freaked out, she would have realized she'd developed cramps in her fingers. "Of course, but-but I don't understand. You're saying the Wizard just sent Ine away … but you don't know where? And that you're in another dimension or something and he's about to send you through some kind of portal to a city near the emperor's tomb?"

The sound of Libby's sobs rattled through the radio. "Yes! And ... and he's giving you guys a choice, that's why he's making me do this call. I don't know anything more than what I'm telling you. You—"

"But why would he *do* that?" wailed Ginny, cutting her off. "None of this makes any sense!"

"Because he's ... I don't know, Ginny, he hasn't told me yet!" returned Libby's voice, and the fear trembling within was so real that Ginny had no doubt this was actually happening, no matter how crazy it sounded. "He says he has everything planned out. But I-I don't think Ine's ever coming back ...." The crackles of the walkie-talkie drowned out the rest of her sentence.

"Libby, you're breaking up. I couldn't hear the last part ...."

"The tomb!" came Libby's voice. "He says it's the only chance you have. I-I think he separated us on purpose so ... so I'll have to do what he says." Her voice broke once more into sobs, and despite all of her apparent effort to stay calm, when she spoke next, her words gurgled out with her tears. "If all of us don't follow his exact instructions, we'll never see each other again! You'll all just stay in this time until you *die* here, Ginny!"

Ginny gulped as she listened to her best friend's voice. "But ... but what about you?"

"Don't worry about me," said Libby, though the words between her sobs sounded anything but convincing. "He-he'll tell me what I have to do. And if I don't mess it up, then I can meet you at the place I described. You—"

Static ripped through the speaker, drowning out the rest of Libby's words. And after several seconds, the radio fell into silence. Still, Ginny held it in her hands. She couldn't let it go. Minutes went by.

And though, as a general rule, Ginny loved little more than being right about anything, this time, being right made her sick to her stomach. She contemplated the walkie-talkie in her hands, remembering that awful feeling she'd had when Libby and Uncle Frank had left on the expedition, and then again later, when she and Sal had first tried to reach them on the radios, but couldn't. She'd *known*, hadn't she? She'd known, and yet she'd still let them go ....

"I just don't understand," she whispered. "And how are we supposed to get there? This tomb place is ... its hundreds of miles away, right?"

Sal chewed his bottom lip as he glared downriver—toward the island and the rapids—though, Ginny considered, there was nothing new to see. Was he in shock? Was he coming up with a plan? Ginny had no idea, and her patience was wearing thin.

"Sal!" she practically shouted. "Please tell me what you are thinking about all this ... this *craziness!*"

Sal turned from the rapids to Ginny. Then he glanced at the deck where the swaths of silk lay. "I'm thinking," he said, "that we'd better hurry up with Plan B. It's our only chance."

15

BENDER OF TIME

"It is possible this has happened before."

Libby peered into the sky, which was thick as spilled ink and pin-pricked with stars. How did she get here? She wanted to cry out, to ask where she was, but her chest felt squeezed flat, as it had in her dream. And all around, there was nothing but the night.

"I am simply trying to answer your question," the Wizard's voice continued, though she could not see him. "You were good enough to follow my instructions on the walkie-talkie call, so I thought I could do you the favor of an answer. You wondered about the bite marks, correct? And times when your interactions with that girl seemed to change in imperceptible ways? It has been on your mind, has it not?"

"Ine," Libby wanted to say, to shout. *"Her name is INE!"* But nothing came out.

"The way time bends, well, it is possible it can loop back on itself. Think about it. If time loops back and intersects itself in the past, then it is also possible that, due to this loop, certain events can play out over and over again, but with minor differences each time. And of course, it is your perception that determines these variations, as you are the co-creator of your own reality. It is a fascinating theory that I have waited so long to toy with …."

"Toy with?" Libby screamed inside, but still, she couldn't speak. She couldn't even move. She wondered if she were inside some sort of stage, like one of those old-fashioned theatres lined with dark, velvet cloth; if so, she wanted to reach out and rip at the twinkling pinpoints of light, rip at the darkness, tear it all down until she could find this horrible man and shred him to pieces. But somehow, she wasn't sure where her hands were ….

The Wizard sighed. "I'm only trying to help. We still have much to cover, but I'm afraid I need us to move along. That's why we are here, after all. You need my help, and I need yours."

"You … need the moonstone," she replied, forcing the words from her mouth, and she was surprised to hear they had sound, that she was now able to speak. "Why?"

"Ah." The Wizard paused. When he spoke again, that annoying calm in his tone had left, and in its place, Libby thought she heard something akin to weariness. "I am sure your Uncle Frank has given you some history of the stone that you wear about your neck? Well, I must confess I may not have been entirely honest with him."

"You ... you mean when you visited him?" It was so difficult to concentrate. "Back in his Flying Tiger days? When you met at a café and played chess?"

The Wizard chuckled but said nothing in reply. Libby glowered into the darkness, feeling so much loathing and misery it was a wonder she could even speak. She couldn't understand half of what this vile man was saying, and all she could think of was Ine. "What happened to my friend?" she finally choked out.

"Your *friend?*" he exclaimed. "She should be the least of your worries! But it is astounding, child. Here you are, floating in decidedly unfamiliar territory—for all you know, we could be just outside Atlantis, for example—, but you're more worried about some pesky little girl?" The Wizard tutted, and though she could not see him, it was as if she could *feel* him, and at this moment, she felt his impatience.

"Well, if it helps, I shouldn't feel too responsible if I were you. As I mentioned briefly, it is entirely possible Ine has been through this before. Now, I've been very cooperative," he continued irritably. "Indulgent, even. On to business, Liberty Frye. Listen very, very carefully; you will need your wits about you. Your fate and the fate of those you love depend upon it, and there is no use going to all this trouble of collecting your mind and body into one place if you're too emotionally feeble to handle it. So are you ready?"

Libby knew it didn't matter whether she was ready or not. Her ears throbbed. Her chest ached. She floated in that darkness, glaring into the abyss that had devoured her friend. She hated him. She knew that now: This man was *evil.* He'd tricked her. And now, she was completely, utterly at his mercy. But she knew he was right about one thing:

She needed her wits about her.

She took a deep breath, feeling the inky air rinse through her as if her lungs were punctured with holes.

"Ready," she said.

The sheets of silk lay in an enormous pile, but slowly that pile started expanding. Ginny watched in amazement as their Plan B took shape, and the shape was that of a giant balloon. According to Sal, it had been Uncle Frank's secret project during their two-month voyage.

"*Semper paratus!*" Sal exclaimed, but for once he said this without a hint of mockery. "Frank was right; you've got to prepare for the unexpected, and while meeting Libby in some far-flung crypt wasn't exactly a situation we imagined, we did consider the possibility that a dirigible might come in handy at some point!"

Ginny regarded the balloon, assuming the bizarre gas-filled blimp was what Sal referred to as a "dirigible." Somehow, the fancy word did nothing to settle the butterflies in her stomach.

"Is it safe?"

Sal grinned.

"On second thought," said Ginny, "don't answer that."

"Extreme situations call for extreme measures!" he replied, as though that statement completely made sense of everything. "And while this wouldn't exactly pass code back home, Frank has come up with a rather ingenious design for isolating the hydrogen! But the best thing of all is that we have an unlimited fuel source because we're converting sea water to gas!"

Ginny noted the various cylinder-shaped converters Sal had lugged onto the deck from the cabin below. According to him, these things sucked up seawater and somehow turned it into hydrogen. Her head spun just to think of it; it was all so incredible it seemed like magic. And it occurred to her that magic and science were awfully related, and while she might not have whatever powers her best friend had in her veins, she did have a head for science.

The thought brought her back to Libby. "So, do you think we have a chance? If this blimp thingy works, can we get there in time?"

"That's the plan, kid," said Sal, but his voice was tight. As if sensing his thoughts, Ginny turned to scan the mountainside. She knew it was far too soon to expect Uncle Frank back—if he would show up at all. For all they knew, he might be stuck somewhere on the mountain, or immobilized by shock.

Ginny gulped in the cool late-afternoon air, forcing that horrible idea from her mind. She just had to focus on the task at hand, and when that task happens to be a giant blimp, it's a pretty hard one to ignore. They'd worked nonstop on it since

Libby's walkie-talkie call, and now it wouldn't be long until they'd be ready for their journey.

"But I just don't get," continued Sal, his gruff voice stretched distractedly, "why the Wizard offered us the choice between staying here … and meeting Libby at the tomb site. Unless he somehow knew Frank and I had been working on the blimp, the choice he gave us is an impossible one. We'd never be able to get there in time!"

Ginny nodded but kept scanning the mountains. There was still so much that she didn't understand, and her head felt like a wobbly mess of puzzle pieces, with nothing fitting together as it should. In fact, all she knew for certain was this:

They had to find Libby, whatever it took.

Even if that meant floating through the sky in a highly flammable hydrogen balloon that had been sealed with some mystery goop of Uncle Frank's invention; even if that meant traveling to an obscure location within a giant tomb complex where, in their own time, was the site of the famous Terracotta Warriors Museum; even if their plan was totally, completely, absolutely crazy (which it was)—even so, they had to try, they had to find her best friend.

But she couldn't help wondering:

Did the Wizard plan this, too? Does he already know what will happen to us, to Libby? And are we just idiots for thinking we have any real choice?

Ginny still searched the mountainside, but in her mind, she imagined one of those wooden mazes—the ones shaped like a large box without a lid—and inside, a little mouse scurried about, bumping into walls and blocked passageways, desperately trying to find the exit. But unbeknownst to the mouse, just outside that box, a fat orange cat waited.

Ginny tried to swallow, but her esophagus felt fossilized. Because it had just dawned on her ....

She was that little mouse.

They all were.

16

THE BELL TOWER OF XI'AN

Libby's eyes flew open.

Wind whipped at her cheeks, and below her, a city spread north and south, east and west. She grabbed the ledge before her, barely trusting her vision. Stone streets lit by red, silken lanterns wove between shops and houses. But she couldn't think straight. Drumming filled her ears, shaking the world with its sound.

Dazedly, she let go of the ledge and stretched her arms outward. They were real. She could see them. And the ledge under her fingertips felt cool and damp from the October mist. The drumming pounded on; had she lost her hearing? Was this what happens when one travels through a portal?

She looked down at the moonstone hanging about her

neck. It still glowed brilliant blue, but it slowly dimmed as if the stone's power had been switched off and the glow was simply residue. Without thinking, she reached up a hand to touch it. It felt faintly warm, which struck her as incredible. Shouldn't it be searing hot? Shouldn't it betray something of its power? She'd just *seen* what it could do:

She'd seen how it had absorbed the portal; she'd seen how that swirling shimmer of silvery grey had grown expansive— the size of a front door, she remembered—only to contract into a thin speck of light that had shot straight into her necklace.

How could it be that something so powerful, so *significant*, could hang so unassumingly around her neck?

The drumming suddenly stopped. She lifted her eyes from the moonstone and realized for the first time that she stood on a tower terrace, and that all around huge red drums and shiny, bronze gongs vibrated from their last impact. A line of men now filed from the terrace to the tower stairway, and she understood she had arrived at the end of some kind of ceremony.

That's right, she suddenly remembered:

Right after floating in that inky darkness, the Wizard had sent her here, to the drum tower. It was dusk. She now stood in the center of the great city of Xi'an, China. And below her, somewhere in the glowing maze of shops and houses and cafes and temples and towers and mosques and pagodas and offices, there was a man who could help.

Hurry, Liberty Frye! We have little time to waste!

She turned to the stairway, slipping behind the last man winding his way down the steps. Dread pricked again at her neck, but she didn't dare stop to wonder at what she was doing. If she had any hope of saving her friends and Uncle Frank, then she hadn't a choice. And it didn't matter if that voice she just heard was real or not; nothing mattered except finding the man and doing what she had to do.

The steps ended and now she stood at the base of the drum tower where an archway opened up to a stone-paved street lined with trees. And setting back from the trees on either side, shops and stalls and restaurants practically burst with activity. She shook her head as if she could shake away her sense of disorientation. The smells of boiling soup and steamed buns and barbecue hit her at once. Her stomach growled in reply.

She entered the street, anxiously glancing about her, but to her relief and surprise she barely attracted notice. A few curious glances flicked her way, but for the most part everyone was so occupied that the sight of a foreign girl wandering the streets made for little interest. And as Libby stepped over the wide, grey stones, she realized this city was entirely different from the sleepy fishing village where she'd arrived only two evenings before. This place was *cosmopolitan*. She'd heard that word used for places like New York or Paris and, looking around, it seemed a fitting description here. There was simply so much *going on*.

Hawkers announced their wares to passersby: brass pots and delicately embroidered satchels; dried fruits and candied nuts; jars of ink; rounds of pressed, dried tea the size of bicycle wheels. Cafes spilled into the street, their tables crammed with diners. Steam billowed from cauldrons and fire blazed under woks. Fresh noodles spun off enormous globs of dough, their spindly shreds perfectly sliced by the millisecond at the hand of a white-aproned chef wielding a silver knife. This place was amazing.

She could barely tear her eyes from the noodle chef, but it was a good thing she did because she practically walked straight into an elderly gentleman who was standing in the center of the street, calmly painting Chinese characters over the stone pavers with a calligraphy brush as tall as Libby.

"Excuse me," she murmured, quickly stepping out of his way, but the man merely nodded and smiled, never breaking a brushstroke.

Libby walked on, half in a trance from all the sights and sounds, half fighting the urge to beg for a steamed bun or a stick of that grilled meat that looked so good she'd shave her head for it. She was starving, and she realized that, for all of the Wizard's toast and tea and boiled eggs, she'd had nothing to eat since early that morning when she, Ine, Uncle Frank and the four men had resumed their journey to the mountaintop.

Libby stopped at a juncture where alleyways snaked to the left and right. More stalls stuffed with trinkets lined these narrow streets, all lit by lanterns that hung from canopies and ornate rooftops, and for a moment she felt so overwhelmed that it was all she could do not to panic.

Look for a teahouse with this sign carved on a wooden board.

That had been the Wizard's instructions, and he'd made her memorize the Chinese characters so she'd recognize them. But as Libby scrutinized the signs from shop to shop, she realized the Wizard had utterly failed to warn her that hundreds of shops and teahouses and who knows what else were packed into these streets—all of them with signs containing Chinese characters.

She turned left down an alleyway, remembering the Wizard had said this particular teahouse stood off the main street and down the first alleyway from the drum tower. She only hoped she'd started from the right tower doorway, because, looking back, she saw now that the drum tower was square in shape, and that it appeared similar doorways opened up to streets on each side. *But no,* she thought, *I followed the line of men down, so the exit I took must be the right one ….*

And then she saw it. She could barely believe her luck. Tucked between a spice shop and a stall selling silk kites, a sign creaked in the breeze over a doorway. *The* sign. She studied it, her heart thrumming in its cage.

And then she stepped toward the door.

※

The *Liberté's* engine rattled below, and before them the river pushed against the ship's hull as they traveled downstream, toward the island and its rapids.

Above them, the oblong, hydrogen-filled blimp tugged through the air. A rudder of sorts was attached to the back of the blimp while cords stretched down from its sides, latching to various places on the ship's deck. Sal and Esmerelda stood at opposite ends of the deck, where two cranks had been installed, waiting for Ginny's signal.

Ginny's heart leapt and pushed against her ribs. She scanned the mountainside once more, but there was still no sign of Uncle Frank. Instead, shadows dug into the riverbank, and soon the countryside would be erased by night.

They didn't have any more time to wait, she knew that; they had to be at the Terracotta Warriors site by tomorrow evening, and they'd waited as long as they could. Uncle Frank would want them to do this, she knew that, too; she knew without Sal ever having to say it. She knew it, but her gut twisted sickeningly inside. She thought she might throw up.

"Kid, we literally don't have all day!" called Sal.

Ginny nodded, but her gaze froze on the island rising from the river to her right. She could feel the rapids now, the tug and pull against the *Liberté*, like invisible talons grasping from a watery grave, greedy for company. And she could hear the pounding of the waterfall just beyond. It was close. Too close. She wanted to change her mind, to turn around. She was suddenly so frightened. She thought she might faint. And what about Uncle Frank? What if they couldn't find him in time?

"Okay," she tried to shout, but her voice shook and cracked all at once. Black splotches exploded in her eyes. Buttercup honked loudly and flapped his wings, then nuzzled up against Ginny's legs as if to comfort her.

"GO!" Ginny tried again and, all at once, Sal and Esmerelda cranked feverishly.

Ginny watched with a pounding heart as, even through her dizzy gaze, she saw part of their deck seam separating from the main ship, like two blocks loosening from each other. The seam widened more and more as Sal and Esmerelda cranked. She couldn't believe they were doing this.

The rapids roared in her ears so loudly she could no longer hear the *Liberté's* engine. And she could feel sprays of water even as they approached the waterfall. From where she stood, she could see the lip of their world pummeling down, down, down into the river below. It was so deep down. A chasm. And everywhere, water spewed and chomped at the air.

Faster and faster. The *Liberté* had never moved so fast before.

"Speed," Sal had explained as he'd shared his plan just before revving up the ship's engine. "It'll help with the impact. As much as I hate to do it, we should destroy what's left behind. Frank's inventions could wreak havoc otherwise!"

"But ... can't we just keep the ship?" Ginny had gulped in disbelief.

"It's too heavy. We can only use part of it for our gondola, which I've already stocked with essentials; everything else has to go."

And now Ginny gawked at the approaching drop-off. In retrospect, she should've insisted on another way. Surely there was another option that didn't involve careening over a waterfall in a giant ship with the hope that their blimp would then lift their deck-turned-gondola from absolute destruction?

There must be another way, but for the life of her, she couldn't think of what it might be.

Ginny shook and shivered. She clutched the deck railing as if it could somehow protect her from what was about to happen ....

The *Liberté* scooted obliviously through the river, faster and faster.

"AHHHHG!" bawled Ginny, but it was too late; their ship teetered on the brink of the waterfall. Seconds felt like minutes as the sickening tilt shifted her balance. Ginny screamed and clutched the railing for dear life; the *Liberté* groaned in reply. Something below the deck where Ginny stood vibrated and tugged, like a giant hand grasping, then letting go. It was the strangest sensation, but even as she watched their ship careen down the waterfall, she felt herself rising into the air.

Despite this sensation of being lifted, Ginny's gaze locked on the river, where water churned against boulders, all spittle and foam. And as the *Liberté* smashed into that fury, it felt to Ginny as if she watched a dear friend being torn to pieces.

17

THE TEA MASTER

L ibby stood in the center of the room.

Two lanterns hung from the carved rafters on each side, lighting the interior with a soft, pleasing glow. Ornate wooden tables with matching stools took up most of the space, but no one sat there; in fact, no one was around at all. The emptiness felt eerie after the bustle outside.

Along the back wall of the room, jars and tins and bricks of tea lined shelves in tidy clusters. A few paintings hung on the empty stretches of wall: waterfalls with misty clouds, a pagoda perched by the side of a lake, an arched bridge over a river shaded by cherry trees.

"Ah!"

Libby spun around to find an elderly man dressed in a

simple robe smiling at her. "I was told to expect you," the man continued pleasantly as if this meeting were a perfectly ordinary event. "Liberty Frye, won't you have a seat? Perhaps some refreshment?"

Libby stumbled backward, her leg thunking against one of the table stools.

"Thank you," she managed, catching her balance, but her voice came out in a whisper. She cleared her throat. Then she sank down to the stool, attempting to appear far more collected than she felt.

The tea master studied her for a moment, his eyes bright and alert under wiry brows. He had a mustache that drooped a bit around his mouth and a long beard that started under his chin, all of it whitened with age. And it occurred to Libby that this man looked far more like a wizard than the Wizard did ….

"I think a bit of silver needle tea, perhaps," the man decided and, with that, bustled to a station in the corner.

Libby watched as the man prepared the tea, her mind too numb from all that had happened to feel surprise at his hospitality. And now that she was seated, she feared if she relaxed anymore she'd fall asleep on the spot. She racked her brain for something to say, if only to stay awake.

"So … how did you learn English?"

The question sounded incredibly dumb once it left her mouth, but the tea master smiled as he poured steaming water into a porcelain pot.

"This place … it is the start of the famous Silk Road, do you not know?" he replied cheerfully. "Have you heard of

Marco Polo, for example? Well, his writings made this city rather famous, but merchants and travelers have been visiting for centuries, long before even his arrival! As a result, many languages are easy to come by. I also speak Portuguese, if you are interested." He winked at her, then resumed his preparations.

Libby stared awkwardly at the table. She definitely needed to work on her languages.

"And ... and the Wizard?" she asked after another moment. "How, er, I mean, if you don't mind me asking ... how do you know him?"

The tea master shuffled over with a tray, now presenting a porcelain cup filled with steaming, amber liquid in front of her. He chuckled and took a seat opposite.

"Excuse me," he said, and then he turned to the back of the room, where Libby noticed a sliding door stood slightly ajar. "Mei!" he shouted, which made Libby jump in her seat—an action she actually found quite helpful because her eyes were beginning to flutter closed. "Where are those dumplings? The child is hungry!" he roared. "As for the Wizard," he resumed in a calmer tone, turning back to Libby, "I have never actually met him. That is to say, not in person."

"But," she reached for her cup and wrapped her hands around it, feeling its warmth sink into her skin. "He said you knew him! And ... and you were obviously expecting me ...."

"Ah, but has your Uncle Frank actually met the Wizard? In *person*? Or did our Wizard present himself much in the same way to your great uncle as he first did to you?"

Libby looked up at him, instantly alert. "How do you know about my uncle?"

"I know whatever the Wizard has deemed important for me to know," he replied. "At any rate, to answer your question, it is in this same manner that I have grown to know the Wizard as well."

"You mean …," began Libby, incredulous, "you mean when my Uncle Frank met the Wizard all those years ago it was through a *dream?*"

"I wouldn't say it is the same as a dream, but it is *like* a dream," the tea master opined with a shrug. "It is a state of being, often best achieved when our minds are relaxed and close to sleep."

"But …."

"It is easy to nod off in balmy weather, is it not?" he continued. "No one else actually *saw* your great uncle meet such a man as the Wizard, did they? And have you considered how they played chess for hours on end, then sat around and chatted for hours more, all in the space of an afternoon? Well, I was not there, so I can only conjecture, but it is my strong assumption that you are one of the very few who has actually … *traveled,* shall we say … to his realm."

Libby thought about that. It was a lot to digest—especially given how much the tea master already knew about Uncle Frank's visit with the Wizard decades ago ….

"It is your great gift, is it not?" asked the tea master, leaning in eagerly as he watched her. "Energy combined with perception? You are able to imagine things that others cannot, which opens up connections in the universe: gaps you can wiggle into—I think that is how the Wizard described it? So you wiggled into a space where the Wizard resides, and that is quite an accomplishment!"

Libby drew back, trying to understand what he meant exactly, but the tea master leaned toward her even more, his eyes growing bright, his voice practically breathless with intrigue.

"Beyond your ability to slip between moments of time and space, can you not sink into the consciousness of others as well? I have heard such things! Or even more incredible, are you not capable of contemplating something with enough fervor that the thought becomes real?"

Libby blinked back at him. "How do you know …?"

"You are a favorite subject of ours," he answered, straightening and placing his hands, palms down, on the table. "A singular possibility of what we all might become … but that will be years and years from now, far beyond my lifetime and even yours. You see, it is one thing to know everything in the universe is made up of energy; energy that swirls and vibrates and combines to form everything in existence. It is one thing to *know* it, and another thing to *command* it."

Libby forgot she was holding her tea; she didn't even feel the heat of her cup burning against her fingers. She felt locked in the intensity of the tea master's gaze, but then he suddenly laughed.

"Ha-ho! I apologize; I do get carried away at times. You were asking about the Wizard. Well, I am afraid I must tell you that our Wizard, for all of his powers, is unable to make himself known in this plane of reality. That is exactly why he needs your help—"

"Husband!" shrieked a voice behind them, which made even the tea master jump in his seat. "You have troubled this girl enough! Can you not see that the poor thing is exhausted?"

An elderly lady, whom Libby assumed must be Mei, scurried toward their table, scolding the tea master as she went: "Such poor manners! Screaming at me like I am your servant, while filling her head with your nonsense! She is but a child, Xue, and one in need of a bath!"

Libby wasn't sure how to feel about Mei's pronouncement; did she really stink that bad? But before she could attempt discretely checking her armpits—or doing anything at all—the woman had her by the shoulders, pulling her with surprising strength from her stool. Libby thought it best to go along, so she rose to her feet and followed Mei through the sliding doorway at the back of the shop.

"Xue knows little else than tea-making and the mad dreams of science," Mei continued to fuss as she pushed Libby into a room. Before her, a wooden tub, like an old-fashioned barrel, steamed in expectation while the faint scent of jasmine wafted in the air. "But rest? The simple needs of children?" Mei snorted with contempt as she looked Libby over. "He knows nothing! Now, shed those dirty rags and into the tub with you!"

Libby blinked.

"A shy one, I see," Mei cackled, marching out of the room. From where Libby stood, she saw wooden panels slide over the open doorway, now covering the space. "Once you are finished, you will have some of my famous dumplings, and then off to bed," she called from the other side of the wall. "Xue will have time enough tomorrow to twaddle on during the journey to the tomb. Have you ever ridden a camel, child? No matter! Believe me, you will be longing for another soak by the time you are through, so enjoy it while you can!"

And with that, Mei shuffled off, leaving Libby to her bath.

Over 700 miles away, Uncle Frank raced down the mountain in his mobile unit.

Hang that Wizard Sheng and the fundamentals of time travel. Hang ethics. Hang everything! The person dearest to him in all the world was *gone*. All bets were off, and if using his hover vent and spider legs would somehow change the course of humanity for the worse, then so bet it.

Besides, he didn't exactly have a choice in the matter. The four men who had carried him up the mountain had run screaming back down it the moment Libby and Ine vanished.

Behind him, one of Liesel Herrmann's companions followed on horseback. His name, Uncle Frank had discovered, was Delun, and he had only come because Liesel refused to leave the spot where her daughter had disappeared. Even when Uncle Frank had explained that there was a possibility—ever so remote, but a possibility nonetheless—that Libby still might be able to be reached, *wherever* she was, on the walkie-talkie he'd left with Ginny, Liesel had only sobbed and waved him away.

"Dear lady!" Uncle Frank had pleaded. "If they are in some other dimension—which I can only assume they are given the circumstances—then a radio might still work! It is our only hope of finding out what happened!"

Of course, Uncle Frank had no way of knowing that, even while he spoke to Liesel of his plan, Libby had already radioed Ginny and Sal at the Wizard's behest. And he had no way of knowing that, from Liesel's point of view, those same walkie-talkies had proven useless just the day before.

He had no way of knowing, until Liesel told him about that last bit. It was more of a scream, actually, as the poor woman railed against Uncle Frank and his friends and all the harm they had caused, cursing them all and their stupid radios that didn't work, which was the whole reason she'd come to this wretched place, and then Liesel turned to the old woman who had accompanied her, and screamed at her as well, cursing the moment, just two nights ago, when the old woman had showed up at Liesel's house, claiming to know the whereabouts of her daughter.

"Leave me!" Liesel had shrieked at the old woman. "I do not know who you are or why you darkened my doorstep, but I don't wish to see your face ever again! Stop tormenting me with your false hopes and unholy ideas. If my daughter has gone to meet our maker, then so be it, but do not suggest any sacrilege of other worlds, other realities! I will not entertain such foolish thoughts!"

And as Liesel yelled and wept, the old woman turned without another word and left them, while Uncle Frank could only sit there, stricken. But then, much to his surprise, Delun stepped forward, suggesting that he accompany Uncle Frank to the *Liberté* and return with any news.

"It is no trouble, madam. And it would be wise to at least try any option …."

And so it was that Uncle Frank now found himself journeying down the mountainside with Delun in his wake. Night closed around them, but Uncle Frank pressed on regardless, his jaw set and his mind ablaze. He found himself muttering out loud like a lunatic, ranting against the Wizard while simultaneously considering various theories as to why Sal and Ginny's walkie-talkie call from the day before had failed, but the whining of his mobile unit and the horse hooves behind drowned out his voice.

"It was the moonstone," he decided, lost in a web of thought. "Liesel said they tried to call around three in the afternoon. It was in that same time frame that Libby had her Incident, so it must have somehow blocked the radio waves … or maybe she *absorbed* them … or perhaps we simply didn't hear it amid the commotion …."

Uncle Frank continued to speculate as the mountainside turned dark. He dared not use his flashlight for fear of draining the battery too soon, but then the clouds rolled from the sky, revealing a half-moon and a splattering of stars that lit their path enough to see.

Delun, who by now had recovered from his shock at seeing what Uncle Frank's special chair could do, took in their surroundings. He peered at the shadowy path before them, silently marveling at this strange misadventure.

He, too, had witnessed the disappearance of the girls. He still reeled from the memory, and his heart ached over Ine. She'd been like a little sister to him; after all, he was the one who had tutored her on their language. How could a girl so alert, so exceptional, so *alive* become nothing, just like that?

He didn't understand what evil had taken place. Nor did he understand his eccentric traveling companion who moved in a mechanical chair, muttering things beyond his comprehension. And he certainly didn't understand the remarkable ship he'd visited before journeying up the mountain, with all its metal gadgets and machines and mysterious swaths of silk.

He glanced again at the stars as if they could offer some sort of explanation, but instead of finding any answers, Delun cried out in alarm.

"What is it?" called Uncle Frank. He turned in Delun's direction, following his gaze, and then instead of sharing in Delun's alarm, Uncle Frank whooped in delight. Excitedly, he reached for his side pack, rummaging around until he found his flashlight, his eyes never leaving the sky. His fingers trembled, but he managed to flick the light on and off in three short flashes, then three long flashes, then three short ones again.

"I'm sending an SOS signal!" he exclaimed to a dumbfounded Delun, and despite all the horrors he'd just witnessed, Uncle Frank couldn't help but laugh out loud.

Because soaring above them in that starlit sky, was part of a wooden ship suspended by a giant balloon.

18

İNTO THE WOOD

Delun watched the blimp rise from where it had temporarily anchored on the mountainside. Moments before, Uncle Frank had clamored into the gondola with his mechanical chair, then waved goodbye.

Delun's mind still spun from all he had seen and heard, especially the news Ginny shared about Libby's walkie-talkie call. And now his shoulders slumped in defeat as the blimp rose higher in the sky, lit from below by the gondola's lights.

After such a taxing journey, he now had to return to Liesel Herrmann with absolutely nothing to offer. While his new friend had hope—however remote but hope all the same—of reaching his grandniece in this tomb of which they spoke, Ine had simply disappeared. No one knew what had become of her. How could he possibly tell poor Liesel that? And yet, he had to.

Delun glanced from the blimp to his saddle bags, now stuffed with fresh supplies of food and water and even a blanket brought from the *Liberté*. He knew his duty, but even so he watched the gondola with a twinge of envy, of yearning, even. He did not understand where these peculiar people hailed from exactly, but he knew it was somewhere not belonging to his world. And now that he'd had a glimpse, he yearned for more. To see more. To *learn* more.

But Delun had a duty to fulfill.

So he raised his hand in final farewell, then turned his horse back to the path that would lead them through the tea plantation and up the stone stairway and to the giant boulder beside the spring and to that wretched, cursed spot where Ine had disappeared.

As Delun journeyed back to Liesel Herrmann, his mind alight with questions and possibilities over all he had witnessed, he could never have imagined that on the other side of the world, *at that exact moment,* a little girl with long, blonde hair and grey-blue eyes whimpered on a forest floor.

When Ine finally got to her feet, it was with resolve. She felt weak and wobbly and scared out of her mind, but she knew she couldn't simply stay where she was. It was much colder here, wherever *here* was, and she knew it would soon be growing dark. Were there animals in this wood? Bad people? She didn't know. She only knew she'd just been sent *somewhere* by the worst person she'd ever met.

She followed a narrow footpath, squinting at the rays of light that beamed through the treetops. Even in her state of shock, she couldn't help but wonder at the sunlight. Shouldn't it be evening by now? Probably seven, maybe eight at night? What kind of strange woods were these?

Ine walked on, and after twenty minutes or so, she found herself in a small village. She blinked in surprise at the little half-timber cottages, the bakery and butcher shop, the stone church. She looked about her, feeling as if she were caught in a dream.

Somewhere in the distance, a bell rang once. *Once.* Ine felt even more confused than before. Was it really one o'clock in the afternoon? Had she fallen asleep without knowing, somehow sleeping through a whole night and the next morning?

Wind whipped through the street, carrying with it a crumpled page from a newspaper. Ine snatched it, her hands shaking from a mixture of fear and exhaustion as she smoothed the paper's surface against the ground. And as she scanned the page, a moan pushed out of her.

Because, no. She *hadn't* slept through the night and into the next day. Rather, instead of being at the end of the day in China, she'd been sent to a faraway place where, on that same day, the afternoon was just beginning.

Had she not been so shocked, the butcher shop and bakery should have already clued her in.

Because she wasn't in China, she was in Germany.

Ine's heart pounded, at first as a flutter, then growing by the second until its booming filled her ears. How did this happen? How could it be possible?

A middle-aged woman wobbled down the steps of the stone church, then stopped short, regarding Ine in surprise.

"Child, where are your shoes?" the woman demanded, and it was only then that Ine realized she had lost her sandals. Her feet were scratched and dirty. They should be cold, too, but Ine couldn't feel it. She couldn't feel anything.

"Child, you look a fright!" continued the woman. "What is your name?"

"Ine." Her reply was barely a whisper.

"What's that? Not your pet name, my dear. I mean your full name. What is it? Where do you live? Where are your parents?"

But Ine realized she had no answer. How could she possibly reply to this woman and be taken seriously? If she told her what had just happened, the woman would think she was insane. She'd be put away. She'd never find a way to get back to her parents again.

The thought sparked a panic inside, electric convulsions that burned and squeezed. As the woman questioned her, now fussing over her torn cape and tangled hair, Ine turned from the woman and ran.

She ran through the street, turning down the lane that led to the little footpath through the woods. She ran and ran, from what or who she didn't exactly know. She just kept running through the trees until she found herself in a clearing. In the midst of this clearing, a stone tower rose into the sky. Just beyond that, she saw a squat, stone hut with a chimney and a wooden door. The place appeared deserted, like the ruins from a time before. Like *her*.

Ine sniveled and wiped her eyes, realizing that tears dripped from her cheeks. She reached into her cape pocket for something to blow her nose with, only to find her spyglass, two smashed duck eggs, a slimy newspaper page … and something else. Something small and round and dripping in egg yolk.

She pulled the object out, letting it roll into the flat of her palm.

Ine hiccupped back another snivel as she glared at the purple berry resting in her hand. And the sight of that thing triggered so much anger and resentment and confusion that she felt as if she might explode. She couldn't believe it. It was as if the Wizard had ensured she'd be left with nothing: no mother, no father, no shoes, no money, no food, no friends, no home ….

Nothing but a stupid, purple berry.

Ine rolled her head back and screamed. And then she formed a fist around that berry and threw it into the wood.

19

ʻTHE ᴀART ʋOF ʀRIDING ᴀA CAMEL

"Time is a river."

"*MEWWAHG!*"

"I beg your pardon?" yelled Libby over the camel's bellowing.

They'd left the ancient city walls of Xi'an behind at least two hours before, and now they traveled between fields of newly-sown winter wheat. Everything around them was flat, with rarely a hill to be seen for miles, so that it felt as if they traveled across a dried ocean bed.

While the endless fields were Libby's view to her left, all she could see to her front was the back of Xue's robe, and if she managed to turn her head to the right between all the wobbling, then she faced Mei, who had insisted on joining them.

Libby grabbed Xue's robe in both fists, desperately trying to stay upright, but the camel's gait threw her back and forth and side to side, and since she and Xue sat between the camel's two humps, her back kept knocking against the second hump each time it moved (a very disconcerting sensation), while her head would thump against Xue's back if she wasn't careful. She felt ridiculous—like one of those bobble-head dolls she'd noticed before on car dashboards. It was all rather distracting.

"Time this and time that," groused Mei, flicking the reins of her own camel. It grunted and bellowed loudly in reply. "It is all my husband thinks of. That, and when he will next visit with his precious Wizard!"

"M-A-W-U-U-U!" groaned her camel.

"A turtle swims along in the river," continued Xue, raising his voice above the noise. "To the turtle, the river he has left behind is the past, though it is still there, still moving. And where he swims currently is the present, though it has depths below that the turtle does not see. And the river before the turtle is the future, though it is one with the present and the past. Still, for the turtle, his direction of travel is one way along the river's current: from his past into his future."

"Tea," decided Mei. "He also cares about tea."

"*EWWAWW!*" agreed her camel.

"*ARRIUUW!*" replied Xue's.

"Imagine the turtle finds a rock in the river," persisted Xue, his voice growing even louder, "just before the top of a waterfall. And as he sits there in the sun, sitting perfectly still in his present and looking into the future, which is the waterfall, a salmon flies straight up in the air from somewhere beyond the waterfall. And as the salmon sails over the turtle, they each make eye contact ...."

Libby chewed her bottom lip, feeling more than a little baffled. She didn't care if time was a river or a turtle or a platypus—it was impossible to follow Xue's lecture between all the *MAAUUUO*-ing and *EWWAWW*-ing and *ARRRIUUW*-ing—but she had the distinct impression that he was waiting for her to say *something*, so she took a stab at it:

"Um, should eye contact be avoided?"

Xue sighed.

"I mean, turtles and salmon don't really mix, do they?" Libby amended hopefully.

"It could be awkward," agreed Mei.

"Nonsense!" roared Xue, but then he seemed to calm down a bit as he heaved another sigh. "You see," he continued in a determined tone, "the turtle *perceives* the salmon as coming from the future, briefly encountering him in his present, and then flying somewhere into the past!"

Libby's head throbbed. She hadn't really slept well in Xue and Mei's house; probably because she was terrified that the Wizard might visit her again in her dreams. Or maybe it was her horror over Ine's disappearance. Or perhaps it was the weight of what she'd realized she'd been doing to her mother. She hadn't had much time to think about it until last night; there'd been so much else going on. But when she'd finally stretched over her mat with nothing but the silence of the room to distract her, it all came flooding back. And now, even with Xue and Mei's constant bickering and the camels' groans and Xue going on and on about a river, thoughts of her mom haunted her; of the knowledge that her mother suffered ... and it was she, Libby, who had inflicted that suffering.

Had her mom known all along? When her hair first started turning white, had she guessed it was her own daughter sapping the strength from her? Draining her life?

A sickening wave in Libby's stomach said:

Yes.

She'd been wrong before to think her mother had been protecting her from Zelna. Her mom had *known*. Libby remembered that night in the cave, when Zelna was destroyed; how her mother had risen up, yelling words she could not understand; words that must have been directed at her own daughter. Somehow, her mom had been fighting that part of Libby that takes over, that part that seemed to rear up when those waves of nausea hit. And later at the hospital and again when they'd finally reached home: the anxious glances cast her way, the feeling there was more left unsaid; the grim resolution on her mom's face. And then, all the laughter and hugs and assurances despite it. All that *love*.

How much had her mother suffered silently while she, Libby, slowly lapped up her life?

Libby gulped in a breath of air, as if she could swallow that horrible feeling of guilt, but it did nothing to stop the questions racing through her mind:

What about what Ginny had told her a few months ago, that night when they were still on the pirate ship? Her heart pounded a little faster at the memory; it was right after the Incident when the moonstones had gathered together into one. Ginny had confessed to Libby that she'd heard her parents arguing over Gretchen's illness once, and that she'd heard them speak of Zelna ....

Well, whatever it was Ginny *thought* she'd overheard, she must have misunderstood, and anyway, considered Libby miserably, if you looked at it the way the Wizard did, then in a way, she *was* Zelna. Or at least she had Zelna's energy. Maybe that's what Ginny heard her mom explaining ....

Libby took deep breaths, fighting the urge to vomit. The swaying of the camel wasn't exactly helping.

"You, Liberty Frye, are like the salmon," continued Xue, oblivious to her torment. "Most of us are like the turtle. A salmon is unique in its ability to travel against the river of time!"

Libby could tell that this was exciting news. Or at least it was to Xue. "Wow," she said, earnestly hoping it was the right response. "That's ... so interesting."

"It is an analogy," sniffed Xue with exasperation. "Just as the salmon expends tremendous energy to battle upriver against currents and eddies and waterfalls, so it is for you. You had to use a different sort of energy to travel *back* in time, and massive amounts of it. Negative energy that causes time to bend against its natural flow. And from what I have been told, you have your very own resource of unparalleled negative energy. Is this not true?"

Libby's skin rippled at Xue's question and the eagerness in

his voice. Whether true or not, she felt absolutely no joy from claiming her own binary star system. In fact, she hated it. Wasn't that the cause of everything bad that had happened? If the Wizard was to be believed, then wasn't this *system* the source of her energy? Energy that takes control over her own mind, that stops at nothing to absorb more and more and more … even the life of her own mother? Who cares if it also made her so powerful she could bend time? What use was that, anyway? So far, it only seemed to end in disaster. If she could choose between time travel and living a normal life with no fear of hurting her mom, there was no question what she'd pick.

Libby's throat was suddenly so swollen she couldn't have answered Xue even if she'd known what to say.

"Leave her alone, husband!" chided Mei. "Can you not see she is distressed enough as it is?"

"I am merely attempting to prepare her," Xue retorted, "for what comes next! So that she may understand! You see," he continued in a gentler tone, "the energy you used to get *into the past* is different than what will be used to go home. To travel into your future merely requires acceleration through the river of time rather than against it. And that, I presume, is what the portal is for. But once you have returned the moonstone to its rightful place in the tomb, it will generate such tremendous energy that, if not properly channeled, could bring disastrous results. Do you understand?"

Libby clamped her mouth tight, fighting a sudden, overwhelming urge to scream at Xue.

Because, no. She absolutely *did not* understand. She didn't understand any of this. She didn't understand how she was supposed to control her own energy; she didn't understand what had happened to Ine; she didn't understand how Ginny and Sal and Uncle Frank could possibly meet her where the Wizard had instructed; and she certainly didn't understand what would happen when she put the moonstone back in its place. She didn't understand anything but this:

She was trapped in the Wizard's scheme, and if she didn't do what he wanted, everyone she cared about would be trapped, too.

"To be honest," she managed to reply, struggling to keep her voice even, "the Wizard didn't explain much; he mostly just told me what I had to do. He only promised that, if I returned the moonstone to the generator, then somehow, it would ... er ... zap us back to our own time. He said we'd all end up meeting at the Terracotta Warriors Museum. I ... I guess its part of the tomb complex, but that the museum part has been excavated in my own time."

"That is all well and good," Xue declared, "but it is the tomb complex in *this* time you should be concerned with. And that is exactly what I am here for! And I must say, it is a great honor to be of service to one such as you. I have waited years for this exact moment! I—"

Their camel bellowed loudly, drowning out the rest of Xue's monologue. But that was just fine as Libby needed the time to think, because soon they would be reaching the site of the emperor's tomb, and then ....

Well, there were a thousand possibilities as to what might happen *then,* and none of them were particularly cheering. For starters, how would she even know where the secret entranceway was? Xue had told her the tomb was vast—larger than many cities, even in her time. Miles and miles of courtyards and streets and offices and palaces, all furnished as though this tomb were a functioning city, with furniture and utensils, tools and weapons, servants and guards, horses and swans—all life-sized statues made of clay and bronze. There were boats and chariots—real ones—and priceless treasures: pearls, gold, precious stones. There were even rivers and lakes—all of it deep in the earth. And there were traps, Xue had warned. If she veered off her path … a shudder went down her back at the thought.

And what if, impossibly, it all went as planned? What then? How could she return home with Uncle Frank and her friends when she knew it would only hurt her mother? She'd be a murderer. How much longer could her mom live when her life was being drained in such a way? Even though it was the last thing Libby wanted to acknowledge, she knew that it all boiled down to this:

She was hurting her mom.

And she didn't know how to control it.

So the only way to stop it would be to activate the portal and send Uncle Frank and her friends back to their own time ….

While she stayed behind.

20

ᴛʜᴇ ʙᴜʀɪᴇᴅ ᴘʏʀᴀᴍɪᴅ

Trees surrounded her on all sides. Most of them were evergreens, and they stretched down the slopes of the hill like bristles on a hairbrush.

But this was no hairbrush.

This was the emperor's tomb.

Or least, it was the top of it.

A chilly breeze swept in from behind Libby, rolling between the pines and tickling their needles, but it wasn't the wind that sent bumps over her arms.

"I am to remind you," called Xue from far below; he and Mei had emerged from the trees moments before, and now they waved their final farewell, "that your magic … it is energy combined with perception. Think of how you perceive things,

Liberty Frye!" And with that, Xue's camel offered an enormous groan as the elderly couple turned their camels and resumed their journey back to Xi'an.

From where she stood on the hilltop, Libby watched them go, her mouth too dry to speak.

What a strange way to say goodbye.

And what did she perceive? She looked around.

She stood at the top of the tomb, now covered from centuries of earth and grass and trees. It was hard to imagine that somewhere below her feet, a giant pyramid pointed toward the sky. But that is what Xue had told her. And all around, fields and uncultivated land stretched as far as she could see. She stood in the middle of nowhere.

"But underneath me," whispered Libby, her voice so tight that it barely came out, "underneath all of this, there is an entire city for the dead."

Her whole body began to tremble; her teeth started chattering. Without thinking, she wrapped her arms around her middle. She didn't like it here, and the abrupt solitude after having spent so much time with Xue and Mei felt disconcerting. And beyond that, Libby realized as she looked around, she hadn't been completely alone since time-traveling over two months ago on her birthday, and now that she finally *was* alone, she felt ill-prepared for it—which was an unsettling sensation for a girl who used to spend entire days hanging out in a tree with nothing for company but a book and a squawking goose ....

The thought filled Libby with an overwhelming feeling of

homesickness. Visions of her life from before wafted through her mind: of their little house that, though small compared to almost everyone else's in town, felt like the coziest, happiest place on earth ... and of her mom, tending to their kitchen garden, growing funny herbs that Libby was just beginning to learn how to use ... and now, her mother was baking her famous breads and cakes and cookies—Libby could practically taste them ... and now, here was her dad coming home after work, his white shirt and tie a little rumpled from the long commute ....

Tears sprang into Libby's eyes, tugging and burning at the edges. She remembered the time her dad had returned home unusually excited; she'd heard her parents speaking in hushed tones in the kitchen about their savings, her dad explaining that they had enough at this point that her mom could open her own bakery in town. "Hasn't that always been your dream, Gretch?"

"But what about you?" Mrs. Frye had replied. "You could use the money to open your own accounting firm so you don't have to drive so far ...."

But then, her mom's mysterious illness kept getting worse, and those hospital tests kept getting more expensive, and then of course, while her parents would never, ever admit to such a thing, the truth was that raising two girls was a lot more of a strain on the budget than just raising one. And so, her dad kept on commuting and the bakery remained a dream ....

Libby scrunched her brows together as she wiped the tears from her eyes. "Stop it," she muttered, forcing her attention back to the hill upon which she stood. She searched the ground with a newfound sense of urgency, looking for any indication of an entrance or lever or even some sort of trap door that would lead to the pyramid below, but there was nothing to see but dirt and grass.

Perception, Liberty Frye.

She tried to remember what the Wizard had explained about perception, but the only thing that came to mind at the moment was the memory of floating through the sky in a library chair, which didn't help one bit. So she turned to the trees.

"Anyone?" she called, and perhaps because she'd already spoken to that chestnut tree while in Qingdao, she now felt strangely comfortable, as if soliciting advice from a grove of evergreens was a perfectly sensible thing to do. "Does anyone here have a clue for me? Anything at all?"

The trees rustled and swayed in the breeze, and it seemed to Libby as if one bent slightly more than the others—almost as if it bowed—but then it straightened once more. Other than that, no answer came. She clamped her jaw in an effort to keep her teeth still and scanned the area again, shifting her feet as she tried to warm herself, when she suddenly felt something hard under her left foot.

Bending down to look, Libby spotted a pebble, barely noticeable where it nested in the grass. It was just a silly pebble, but her mind drifted again to what Xue had said:

Perception.

Libby bent lower to grab the pebble, only to discover it was buried deeper than she thought. She got on her hands and knees and started digging the soil from around it until she could jiggle it loose, and when her fingers could reach around the pebble to pluck it from the ground, she found that instead of plucking, she had to pull.

Libby dug her heels into the ground and tugged against the pebble with all of her might. She pulled and pulled—she didn't know for how long—when the ground quite unexpectedly began to shudder and shake, knocking her off her feet. She yelped and scuttled backwards as the earth yawned open, just inches from her toes, and she watched with startled amazement as the pebble rolled into the yawning gap and disappeared into the depths below.

She continued scrambling backwards as the ground moaned and shifted under her, shaking the whole hillside. It was as if a giant sleeping for centuries had just been jostled awake, and then, before she could even get on her feet, that gap in the earth yawned wider, like it was stretching its skin, forming fissures that snaked through the earth, this way and that. Libby didn't know where to scuttle, it was all happening so fast, but in the next moment a fissure flicked her way ... and swallowed her whole.

Down she went, sliding on her back, her heels kicking at the ground with nothing to grip at, nothing to push against. The air smelled dank and foul, but that was nothing compared to the terror of falling through utter darkness.

Then she landed on something that bounced her straight up in the air, before gravity pulled her back down again. This time, the bounce wasn't as extreme, and as she sat there numb with shock, she wondered if she'd landed on some sort of ancient trampoline. She didn't know, but whatever it was she scrambled off, feeling with her feet for the ground, and it wasn't until she was standing that she noticed her moonstone glowing faintly, though it was no match for the tomb's veil of shadows.

Through the haze, she made out a passageway that hooked around the corner. She stepped toward it, forcing her feet to do her will.

She must be in the center of the mausoleum, she considered, her mind careening with a million thoughts. From what Xue had explained, though the emperor's underground city stretched for miles in each direction, the pyramid that stood above his actual tomb formed the centerpiece. If one tried to enter this fortress from the east or west, north or south, disaster was sure to meet them, for the emperor had laid traps in wait for anyone who dared trespass.

Libby stepped forward, now holding her moonstone before her to maximize its light. A blue glow quivered over the earthen floor and walls that immediately surrounded her, but there was nothing else to see but the pitch black all around. She felt blind, with no way of knowing what waited ahead. She tried to focus on her breathing—even though the taste of the air disgusted her—in and out, trying to keep her breath steady, and she suddenly wished Ginny was with her, because she could now state unequivocally that it was so much scarier to face a creepy underground tunnel all alone ....

But that was selfish. She should be glad Ginny wasn't here.

What if she walked into one of those booby traps? A single misstep might trigger automated crossbows, skewering her on the spot with arrows. Or what if these walls began closing in and crushed her like a grape? Snakes? What about snakes? Or spiders? The thought made her tremble, sending the moonstone's glow shuddering eerily about, which did nothing to ease her anxiety.

She walked on, the passageway curved and sloped gently downward, and with each of her steps the moonstone's glow grew brighter. And just as Xue had explained, she also felt a tug, similar to when she'd left Sabine's hut on a bicycle almost a year ago and been pulled into the woods where Ginny hid. It was like that, but not as strong.

"Follow the stone's pull," Xue had instructed. "It will lead you to its resting place."

The twisting and turning finally stopped, and now Libby found herself in a narrow, rectangular room. Doorways stood on each side, but her moonstone tugged to the right, so she followed its pull in that direction.

As she walked on, the moonstone pulled with more and more force, so that soon she found herself practically dragged through the various rooms and twisting hallways, passing statues and storage chests and even piles of bones.

The moonstone tugged harder and harder; she felt as if her feet couldn't keep up. She was running, panting and sweating as the moonstone rose up in the air, pulling her forward with its chain, yanking against her neck. Faster and faster, she ran through the labyrinth.

Until she slammed straight into a wall.

Libby gasped for breath as the moonstone banged against the wall as if trying to break through it. She raised her hands to push away from the wall, her fingers digging into centuries of dust and debris, and it wasn't until then that she felt a seam stretching up the wall from the ground to the ceiling.

She felt along the seam; she was sure the wall must be some sort of door that slid open, but she couldn't find a way to do it. The moonstone continued to pound, and Libby's brain pounded with it. Surely there must be a way; the Wizard wouldn't have sent her this far just to fail now.

Then she remembered:

"Öffnen," she blurted desperately. "Öffnen Vindulvian!"

A great rumble came in reply. Libby stumbled backward.

And then, the wall groaned as it split apart.

21

RIVERS OF MERCURY

Zoom! The moonstone yanked Libby through the parting wall.

She stumbled forward, jerking and slipping over the floor as the moonstone amulet pushed through the air like an arrow, pulling her in its wake.

She found herself in a small room with no windows, no doors and no other exit other than the sliding wall she'd just come through. All around, carvings crept over the walls: figures of animals and spirits, flowers and trees, writings made up of characters she could not read, but they glowed eerily in the amulet's increasingly bright light.

The amulet pulled her toward a rectangular, stone structure that rose from the center of the room. Long steps wrapped around the structure so it looked like a mini pyramid, but without the pointed top.

A pyramid within a pyramid.

She was at the actual grave—the emperor's tomb, thought Libby. It had to be.

But the moonstone didn't stop there. It pulled her toward the steps instead, then up again, so that Libby found herself scrambling up the tomb's stairs until she reached the top.

Banging and banging, the moonstone smashed against the top of the ornately carved slab. Dust and fragments of the stone slab exploded into the air. Libby choked as she scrambled on her hands and knees, frantically feeling along the surface for any seam, any sign of where it might open, but nothing could be found.

"*Öffnen Vindulvian!*" she shouted, but this time, no rumble came in response, no movement.

The moonstone continued to pound. What else could she do? Whatever it was after, it must be something below the surface of the tombstone, but the slab was so big—at least eight inches thick, and much longer and wider than her—there was no way Libby could move it. She tried anyway, pushing with all her might, but of course nothing budged.

The moonstone continued to pound, its chain twisting painfully against her neck, but she dared not risk taking it off. She knew she had to keep it on; she couldn't let it go, not until she'd found its home.

She bit back a whimper and lowered herself to the tombstone, rolling on her back so that the amulet stopped tugging and instead pressed against the slab's surface like a magnet. She wondered if the chain had cut through her skin—surely it must have—but she was so grateful for the reprieve from the tugging that she didn't raise her hand to check, she just lay there, feeling the painful throb slowly leave her neck.

Silence settled around her. The blue glow of the amulet flickered over the wall's carvings, and straight above where Libby lay, she could see etchings on the ceiling: carved stars and mystical symbols, and it seemed as if those stars floated in the sky, and all around her, the walls of the room gave way to twisting trees, the dank tomb air changing into the piney scent of forest ....

"You have done well, child."

Libby felt her body twitch. Had she fallen asleep? What just happened?

"Yes."

She knew that voice. It sent a shudder through her, but she couldn't find her arms to wrap around herself.

Libby groaned. Not again. She didn't want to face him, to hear from him. She didn't want to see him, not ever, ever, ever. She just wanted to finish her task and get this over with. At such an important juncture, how could she have possibly fallen asleep?

"But what do you *perceive*, child?"

Libby swallowed down the resentment she felt gurgling inside. She tried to focus.

"That ... I'm stuck inside a room. A crypt, I guess," she answered, trying to stay calm. "The moonstone, it pulled me to the top of this stone pyramid thing. I think it's the actual grave of the emperor. I think it wants to go down *into* it, but I don't know how ...."

"Have you tried?"

"Of *course* I've tried!" She was surprised to find herself yelling. "What do you think? That I'm hanging out with-with *skeletons* for the *fun* of it?"

When the Wizard spoke again, the patience in his voice was gone.

"Obviously, you have not tried. Not entirely. If you had, you wouldn't be taking a nap! Do you recall nothing of our talks? Nothing of Xue's teachings?"

Libby felt her hands ball into fists at her sides. She couldn't *see* them, but she could feel them. She wanted to punch the Wizard in the face. She couldn't see him, either, but that didn't change the urge.

"Think of your powers," pressed the Wizard. "Remember? We're all just a collection of zipping, zapping particles. And deeper still, we're all just energy. All of us. Everything. If you can just imagine it, you will also see the gaps. Gaps to wiggle into."

Libby tried to focus on her breathing. She lay there, somewhere between the tombstone and her mind, paralyzed by this horrible dream-world where the person she despised the most could reach her, torment her. Her breath came in quick bursts, in and out, in and out. She hated him so much.

"Open your eyes."

Libby's eyes flew open. Against her back, she felt the engravings of the tombstone's slab. And what was the slab made of? Stone. Stone, like the granite in the mountains; all that energy she had felt that day, throbbing inside ….

She considered the Wizard's words; about how her skin and the tunic she wore and the stone slab beneath her were all really made up of the same things, just different combinations. She imagined that if she looked very, very close, she'd see bright, bouncing particles, jiggling and zapping like rubber balls, and the spaces between them ringed with energy. She imagined zooming in deeper still, within each of those rubber balls, and she saw more space, more gaps, more folds and wrinkles, more … *energy*. She felt it pull at her; or was she pulling at it? Could she sink into it? Through it? The slab that pressed at her no longer pressed. She was a part of it. *It* was a part of her.

The world went black.

The blue glow of the amulet was gone, and in its place, she saw nothing. But she sensed *everything*.

Was she falling? Libby reached out to push herself up, but the slab was no longer below her. Nothing was. And then, just as quickly, her feet hit the ground. It took her a few seconds to steady herself, but when she'd calmed down enough to take in her surroundings, she saw that her moonstone once again glowed blue.

With trembling hands, Libby touched the walls to her right and left—walls that *hadn't been there* just moments before. And the chamber in which she stood was much, much narrower— more like a tunnel maybe. Or … Libby caught her breath as the realization hit her:

More like a grave.

Libby exhaled, air shuddering out of her as she looked around, still not quite believing she'd just achieved the impossible … that she'd somehow traveled *through* the slab of the emperor's tombstone! But there was no mistaking the fact that the crypt and the pyramid upon which she'd rested were gone, and before her, lit by the glow of her amulet, a narrow passageway sloped upward.

But before Libby could determine if she was standing on any bones or disintegrated body parts, the moonstone yanked her forward with excruciating strength. She raced up the sloping ground, now scrambling on hands and knees, then back on her feet as she ran through another chamber, this one perfectly round and surrounded by enormous doorways shut tight against the outside. Above her, a domed ceiling glittered with gemstones and pearls.

Faster and faster she ran. She didn't know where she was going, but when she looked down, she became frightfully aware that she traveled over a narrow pathway, one of several that stretched from each doorway toward a platform in the center of the chamber, like spokes on a wheel. And in the center of this platform a strange and twisty object rested, while churning below the narrow pathway where she ran, on either side, something silvery and liquid flowed, like rivers of mercury.

And then she was at the platform in the center of the chamber, face-to-face with the strange object. It appeared to be an oblong boulder, but with all kinds of peculiar twists and crevices in its body—like a contorted octopus—and at the top of the boulder, just shoulder-height to Libby, a central spire pointed upward. And below the oblong body, tree-root-like tangles twisted this way and that, sinking into the stone platform and disappearing below.

Even as Libby took in this peculiar apparatus, the moonstone flew forward and slammed into a crevice that perfectly fit the shape of the amulet. And then everything—the moonstone and the boulder-thing it had lodged into—glowed brilliant blue, lighting up the entire chamber. Whirring filled her ears.

Libby scrambled at the chain about her neck, slipping her head out from underneath it, and as she did so, she realized that the boulder must be the tomb's power source Uncle Frank had once mentioned—like a generator, more or less—because now she saw that it was *moving* the room, round and round.

Everything in the room spun: the platform and generator one way and the walls the other. The room was but a blur of blue and a humming sound that echoed off the walls.

But then the spinning suddenly stopped. Groans rattled around her as the chamber's doors rolled open, moving up from the ground and disappearing into the ceiling above. Libby gripped the spire of the generator, feeling decidedly off-balance, as the smell of something familiar hit her nose.

Then she realized:

The river below her wasn't mercury. At least, it wasn't anymore. It was … water! It smelled of river water mixing with sea water, that churning, brackish scent—like the air sometimes smells on windy days right before a storm—its smell quickly filling the chamber as the water rose and rose.

As if that wasn't confusing enough, Libby noticed that the spoke-like walkways connecting the doors to where she stood had disappeared during all the spinning, and now the stone platform rumbled and rose from the swirling water. A wooden deck appeared beneath the platform, the water pouring over its sides into the churning below. Then a mast and an ornate, rectangular sail creaked up from the deck, like a fallen tree resurrecting, and as the deck continued to rise from the water, Libby could see that she actually stood at the center of a wooden, Chinese boat!

She didn't have time to process this remarkable turn of events because just then, a roaring wind curled through one of the opened doorways. The boat rocked and groaned in reply as brilliant blue light beamed everywhere: bouncing off the ceiling, filling the chamber's space, gushing out the open doors, reaching down, down into the water, tendrils of brilliant blue twisting like electric eels.

And then the boat lurched forward, whisking Libby through one of the doorways.

22

ᴛHE ʟABYRINTH

Ginny peered at the earth far below. Fields spread into hills that grew into mountains. On their right, some distance away, a river cut through the countryside. At first, this had been the Yellow River. They had followed it through the night and into the morning.

And then, a few hours after the sun stood directly overhead, Sal spotted the tributary they'd been looking for. "There it is!" he exclaimed. "That's the Wei River, branching off from the Yellow! Not much longer, folks, and we'll be at our destination!"

But that had been almost three hours ago. The sun now tilted to the west, so that the waning afternoon light glowed into their faces. Despite Sal's optimism, there was still nothing in sight that looked like their Terracotta Warriors location. Ginny shielded her eyes as she chewed her lip nervously. She didn't know the precise time for sunset, but it wasn't far away. And even with their solar lights, she knew spotting their exact location would be tricky in the dark ....

She glanced over at Uncle Frank, who had been studying his navigational charts for the past three hours with alarming intensity. Much to her relief, he finally put them down.

"Time to head south, toward that rise," he announced, pointing to where the land rose up from the river plains.

Ginny followed his gesture and peered dubiously below. "But there's nothing there! Where's the tomb? The creepy stuff?"

Uncle Frank harrumphed. "It's all underground, Ginny. It isn't for another hundred years that some shards of clay will be discovered, which will eventually lead to digging up part of the land and uncovering the Terracotta Warriors. But most of the emperor's tomb remains unearthed, even in our own modern times."

Ginny thought about that as she regarded the countryside below. It was hard to wrap her head around the fact that in the future, there was a museum somewhere down there, with these clay Warriors nicely displayed for public view. She imagined people showing up and paying for a ticket; maybe they'd even have a cafeteria and one of those informational movie theatres. There would be roads and parking lots and signs and walkways. There would be guidebooks, even.

Their gondola twisted as Sal steered the blimp, bringing Ginny back to the present ... or technically, wasn't it the past?

The thought made Ginny's mouth pucker in annoyance. She'd had enough of this philosophical nonsense; she was ready to get back to her *own* time where the present was *actually* the present and the past was *actually* the past and the future was *actually* the future and not her present as she perceived it while being trapped in the past .... Oh good grief! Ginny glared at the earth below. She couldn't even get it straight in her head! This whole time-thing was utterly pointless, and besides, the only thing that mattered at the moment was getting to the underground Terracotta Warriors site *today*—no matter if *today* was technically the past or the present or the future—and before dark.

The River Wei now curved away as they headed toward the hill Uncle Frank had pointed out earlier, and she felt their gondola lowering in altitude; the wind pushed into her face and whipped at her hair. "But ... how do we know we've got the right spot?"

"Because you've got me," said Uncle Frank, forcing a smile. It didn't do much to comfort her. "I've been mildly obsessed with the emperor and his tomb ever since I met the Wizard all those years ago. I've kept anything I could get my hands on about excavations, recent discoveries, you name it. So you see that hill directly below us?"

Ginny glimpsed again over the railing to where the cone-shaped hill covered in trees peeked up from the fields, and nodded.

"That, I believe, is where the pyramid is. And within that pyramid, the emperor's tomb resides. It's part of a huge underground complex. Right now," he added ominously, "Libby must be down there somewhere."

His words sent bristles over Ginny's arms and legs; her skin felt as if it were shrinking over her bones. She shivered but kept her mouth pressed tight together, not daring to ask the less-than-optimistic questions popping through her mind. Questions like: Did Uncle Frank really believe Libby could be transported from some invisible dimension into the labyrinth of tombs below? Would she know where to go in such a maze? How would she possibly find them? And did he trust the Wizard?

"And … and the Terracotta Warriors?" she asked instead. "Are they in there, too?"

"Almost." Uncle Frank pointed to where the land flattened out again. He cleared his throat. "We're headed there. If I've calculated correctly, the Warriors' excavation site and museum would be just under a mile from the main tomb. It's all connected underground, of course …."

The gondola glided over the hill and now lowered slowly to the earth, Esmerelda and Sal carefully letting out hydrogen from the blimp so it descended in increments. The gondola sank lower and lower as the field below drew closer. But it was still just an empty field. How could this ordinary, in-the-middle-of-nowhere place be the right spot? She turned to Uncle Frank, watching his face closely. *Was he sure?*

Their gondola hit the ground, then skipped up a foot or two before bumping to the ground again, jostling everyone inside. Ginny barely noticed.

"It doesn't look like much," grunted Sal, hobbling out of the gondola with a rope in one hand.

Ginny gulped in agreement as she looked around. She thought again about that last walkie-talkie call, when Libby had instructed her to be at the site of the Terracotta Warriors by evening the next day. At that time, Ginny had imagined something a bit more ... well, terracotta-like. Or warrior-like. Or even crypt-like. In fact she'd imagined pretty much *anything* but an open field in the middle of nowhere. Her heart raced uneasily.

"So what do we do now?"

Uncle Frank checked his charts once more. Then he glanced to the west, where the sun slowly slipped behind hills surrounding the river plain. He took a deep breath.

"Now," he said, his voice thin, as if it were squeezed down and coming apart at the edges, "now we wait."

❀

But they were not the only ones waiting. A mile away and deep underground, Libby held on tight to the generator's spire as the boat hurtled through chamber after chamber. Blue light beamed everywhere; it twisted into the walls and through the water like blood vessels, stretching and growing, illuminating everything it touched.

The boat sailed into a wide, open hall filled with life-sized clay dancers, all in various postures as though in the middle of a performance. Zipping past them, Libby was almost certain that she spied them *moving*, their clay-formed arms and legs stretching before their bodies as if awakening from a deep sleep, their hair waving in the water like strings of seaweed ....

But then the boat rocketed through what looked like a main gate, leaving the dancers behind. Here and there, Libby detected bones bobbing in the water—once she was sure she saw an entire skeleton. She gripped the spire of the generator harder as the boat whooshed through another complex where clay and bronze horses stood beside chariots, all lined up in tidy rows. Water surged over everything, knocking the horses and chariots out of formation and whisking them to the surface. But wait! The clay horses were transforming into *real* horses ... hooves pawing, nostrils flaring ... they neighed and snorted at the water crashing all around.

Libby could only watch helplessly as the ship pushed out out of the stables and traveled over a vast, open space. In front of her, a network of tunnels branched this way and that, and the water tumbled into a tunnel to her left, carrying the boat along. It felt as if she traveled upward, but of course there was no real way to know, before the tunnel suddenly opened into a chamber of sorts. Before her, a wide staircase led to a pedestal where huge rings of multi-colored light swiveled this way and that—red and yellow and green and blue and violet—like hula hoops swirling around a giant, invisible ball.

The water surged toward the pedestal, rising over the stairs, carrying the boat, higher and higher, until Libby was eye level to the swirling rings of light.

And then, the swirling rings vanished. In their place, a pillar of white light throbbed. The boat shuddered to a stop a few feet away, and the sudden shift from movement to stillness was jarring. Libby blinked as she released her grip on the generator's spire and looked around.

The glowing blue water remained around her, but the tempest had stopped. No wind, no roar, no movement. Wherever she was, it was quiet. The generator still hummed, but in a gentle way, like the steady buzz of electricity through cable wire, while before her, the pillar of light slowly faded. A shadow flickered somewhere within, and as the light grew fainter, the shadow grew more defined … until the next thing Libby realized, the shadow was no longer a shadow.

It was a man.

He turned to face her. His skin sagged in folds from his eyes, his hair wild and wispy and so faded with age it hardly had any color at all, his shriveled mouth barely a line across his face. And when he spoke, his voice seemed to scratch at the air, like dry grass in the wind.

"Welcome, child," the man said. "I have waited so long for your arrival."

23

A World of Dreams

The man stepped forward, then forward again, reaching for the generator where Libby remained by its spire. She stumbled backward, her feet leaving the stone platform and clunking onto the wooden deck.

"I won't hurt you, child. I just need the moonstone."

Libby clutched the deck railing behind her, too stupefied to move further away.

"You don't recognize me?" He shook his head and tutted. "A pity. I *was* rather dapper back in the day. Well, I must say, if you suddenly aged a few millennia all at once, you wouldn't look so great yourself."

Even in her state of shock, the meaning behind his words took shape. "You mean, you're …?"

"The Wizard, child, yes."

And with that, he reached toward the generator and plucked the moonstone from where it nested. Immediately, everything fell into darkness; everything but the pulsing blue glow of the stone. It flickered over the Wizard's face.

"I … I don't understand," she managed to say, but her voice, barely a whisper, echoed off the chamber walls, sending it reverberating back, like dozens of ghosts hissing in the darkness.

The Wizard merely perused the boat deck, lifting the moonstone so that its glow spilled before them. "Isn't there somewhere to sit? I am uncommonly tired."

Still shaking, Libby pointed to her left, where a built-in bench rested between the deck and railing.

"Ah! That's right." The Wizard shuffled over and lowered himself to the bench. "Much better. Now, I suppose the first thing I should do by way of thanks is to explain what just happened."

Libby could only stand there and stare.

"Shall I get to it?" he asked delicately, as though suspecting Libby had grown rather feeble-minded, and when she still didn't answer, he cleared his throat and continued. "I told you I wasn't entirely honest with your Uncle Frank all those years ago. Do you recall?"

She remembered to nod.

The Wizard smiled, the blue glow of the moonstone lighting his mouth, his nose, the paper thinness of skin crinkling across his cheeks. "Then allow me to tell you another story …."

❀

CHAPTER 23

Many, many years ago, there lived a Wizard. He lived on a beautiful island, untouched by humankind. But the island was also solitary, so the Wizard often traveled to the mainland, where he could interact with others (should he so wish) and obtain items of his desire.

On the mainland, the Wizard had a favorite spot nestled in the mountains, where freshwater springs gurgled from slabs of rock. Here, the wind swept away all woes of life, and everything around and beyond and beneath gathered into a well of energy—energy that the Wizard could harvest at will ....

"The-the mountain near Qingdao?" croaked Libby, her voice still barely a whisper, yet the sound of it made everything feel more *real*—as though the recent journey through underground chambers ... and the vanishing rings of light ... and the electric blue water all around ... and the materialization of an antiquated Wizard ... and the gazillion other bizarre things that had occurred since sliding down a chasm and landing smack dab inside an ancient pyramid were all perfectly natural occurrences, and nothing that a good chat couldn't sort out. "The one I hiked to?"

"Yes, child, *that* mountain. Must you interrupt? Obviously, I am the Wizard of which I speak."

"Sorry."

The Wizard drew a deep, rattling breath. "Because of this unique place, I was able to extend my life beyond that of any other mortal. I lived off of this energy for hundreds of years, growing wiser and wealthier and skilled in many things. As time passed on, my name was whispered through the villages below, my renown growing throughout the Kingdom. Though very few had ever met me, I was now famous; an immortal sage who knew the secret to eternal life."

"And … that's how the emperor found out about you?"

The Wizard threw her a sour look, the blue light wobbling against his chin and mouth. "Do you realize how long I have waited to actually *speak* to a person, flesh-to-flesh? These interruptions barely allow me to hear my own voice!" He sniffed. "Fine. In any case, you are correct: that is indeed how the emperor found me. The trouble was, I dared not share my secret with him. If I told him, I had no doubt the emperor would make his new home atop my precious spot, taking my source of energy for his own. That simply would not do.

"Fortunately, I had an inkling that another source of energy existed, though in a different form. If my suspicion was correct, then this new source would be far more concentrated—thus, capable of things I had only dreamed. So I offered up the knowledge of this stone in the Himalayas, thinking it would at least distract the emperor long enough to leave me be. But not a year later, he was once again on my doorstep, this time with a caravan of men and horses … and a giant chunk of glowing blue rock."

"The moonstone," murmured Libby.

The Wizard sighed.

"Quite so—that is to say, it was the moonstone and the rock that surrounded it." He nodded toward the generator. "And now, the emperor demanded results. After all the journeys and sacrifices and years spent in search of eternal life, now that he had a source, how could he harvest its power? He assured me that if I did not help him—"

The Wizard broke off into a spasming cough. When he spoke again, it seemed to Libby that he looked even older than before; his skin sagged from every bone on his body—like sheets on a hanger. She wondered if it were possible for him to literally melt away.

"Well, it doesn't really matter what he threatened, does it?" he wheezed. "You see, I could have eluded the emperor; I could have hidden from him or otherwise escaped his tyranny, but now that I had such an eager subject, I was determined to take full advantage."

Libby watched him as he spoke, the shock from all she'd just witnessed slowly subsiding. "What do you mean?"

The Wizard eyes glinted in the moonstone's light. "Due to my studies, I knew of a certain possibility that had never before been tested, but could, in theory, create exactly what the emperor was after. So I told him all about it—I confess I may have taken liberties with certain facts, but the important thing is that he agreed to my plan."

"What … what plan?"

"Patience, child." The Wizard raised a hand, then let it drop, his fingers once more gripping the moonstone. "We set to work. It was a long-standing custom for rulers to prepare elaborate mausoleums for their afterlife, so all the emperor had to do was ensure that everything he wished to enjoy for the rest of eternity would be in this same necropolis with him. In the meantime, I applied my skill to the Himalayan rock, creating the generator you now see and carving the heart of it into the moonstone I hold in my hands."

Libby glanced at the stone glowing against the Wizard's lap where he held it. Blue light eked between his fingers and highlighted the thin flesh of his hands, glowing through his skin so that his veins pulsed like candescent spider webs. And yet, despite the stone's obvious power, she realized the generator must have affected its pull, because now, the stone sat still in the Wizard's hands, with no signs of the violent tugging that had wrenched so painfully at her neck.

"Once the generator was complete," resumed the Wizard, "I made a few runs myself. Through the power of the moonstone, I was able to transport myself into dimensions I'd never before experienced, never even knew for certain they *existed* until that moment. In one of these, I began building a city for the emperor; it was much easier to do such things in this place. I needed no craftsmen, no architects, no materials, even. All I needed was my imagination. And so I built a beautiful world there, filled with palaces and rivers, birds and beasts, art and such luxuries I have never enjoyed on earth. A world of dreams! I also built beautiful dwellings for each of the emperor's servants, his entertainers—even his army."

Libby inhaled sharply, realizing she'd been holding her breath. "And ... and then?"

"And then the moment came for our plan to be executed. The emperor staged his death, drinking in vials of certain extracts I'd instructed him upon. Finally, he was carried to the giant tomb complex he'd spent his whole life building, accompanied by those he most favored. As part of the ceremony, this necropolis was surrounded by his military, and all his horses and animals and remaining entourage were brought to various locations he'd built for them to pay final homage to their great leader."

The Wizard broke into another convulsion of coughing, and as he choked and sputtered, Libby noticed he gripped the moonstone tightly between both hands. And it almost seemed as though some of the stone's blue glow wasn't just highlighting those spidery veins of his, but actually going *into* them ....

"Well," the Wizard continued in a rasp, "the emperor wasn't dead, of course. Not yet. And when I placed our moonstone into the generator, it created an enormous surge of energy that sealed the entire tomb complex and carried the emperor to his new world."

"To the one you created?" breathed Libby, still not quite believing. "The one in another dimension?"

A twitch lifted the Wizard's left cheek, a hint of a smile mixed with bitterness. He bent his head in affirmation. "Precisely. But it wasn't just the emperor who made this extraordinary journey. Exactly as we'd planned, all those unwittingly gathered at his tomb were to be transported as well. Servants who stood grieving by his supposed corpse suddenly found themselves kneeling before him in his new world. So, too, his artisans, entertainers, relatives ... well you get the general idea."

Tingles went up Libby's spine as she stood there, listening to this fantastical tale unfold. "And then?"

"Of course the sheer *amount* of individuals to be brought with him was astonishing. Alas, due to … an unfortunate incident … not all of them made it. Some were left entirely behind, some were caught midway through the process—their forms not quite leaving this world and never quite reaching the other. An entire army of soldiers, for instance." He gave her a sly wink. "Those are your Terracotta Warriors, by the way."

Libby shrank from the deck railing, her eyes still locked on the Wizard. "You mean that … the clay soldiers … they were actually *real people?*"

"Not just the Warriors. Did you not see things come to life during your journey here?"

Libby suddenly realized she was leaning against the generator. She jumped away, grabbing the deck railing again to steady herself.

The Wizard nodded in understanding. "You see, when you activated the generator once more, you switched the process, bringing the life force of those caught in-between, back. Well, almost. You saw how I stopped the generator by removing this?" The blue light flicked across his eyes as he lifted the stone from his lap.

Libby gulped and nodded.

"That stopped the transference. I do not believe the moonstone's power has touched most of the tomb as of yet. Our Warriors, for example, should still be standing in their clay formations. As for those that *have* returned, I fear their mortal bodies will not last long in this world. They will turn to dust, as will all of us eventually."

Libby shook her head. "But I still don't understand how ...."

"Ah!" cut in the Wizard, squeezing the moonstone even tighter in his hands. "I forget myself. That's what eternity does to one's wits, child. What I *should* have explained is this:

"Just as I stopped the transference today, so it was that over two thousand years ago, *someone else* stopped the transference before the process was complete. And that part," he concluded with a weary smile, "is what I've actually been truthful about."

Libby's mind yanked this way and that, pulling together bits and pieces of information. "Are ... are you talking about what you once told Uncle Frank?" she guessed, remembering Uncle Frank's story on her birthday, when he'd explained the history behind the moonstone. "About his friend Lam, and how Lam's relative stole the moonstone from the tomb?"

This seemed to please the Wizard. He nodded, briefly closing his eyes. "You see? Even lies hold truth in them; the trick is knowing where to look! It was indeed an ancient relative of Lam's," he continued in a wheeze. "He must have been a worker in the tomb who, unbeknownst to me, had witnessed the generator's power. He must have planned ahead of time, devised a secret escape route, but in any case, on that fateful day, I had agreed to accompany the emperor to his new world; to 'show him the ropes' ... I think that is how you would say it? I never intended to *stay* there. Goodness! With that dreadful person?"

"So ...," cut in Libby, her mind racing so quickly that she grabbed at her thoughts, trying to put them into words before new ones took their place, "you were in this world with the emperor when Lam's relative stole the stone from the generator, leaving you stuck there … forever?"

"Can you imagine?" The Wizard leaned forward, his expression almost eager, as if he were confiding a great secret over tea and crumpets with a close friend. "And when the emperor discovered that everything he had wished and planned for had not made it, he became furious beyond words."

Libby squeezed her eyes shut, then opened them again. "So … you've been stuck in that world for over two thousand years, right?"

"You are beginning to see!" replied the Wizard, beaming up at her in that alarmingly familiar way. It made Libby's skin crawl, and all the horrible things he had done came flooding back: of what he'd done to Ine, of what he'd done to Uncle Frank and her friends, of what he'd done to *her* ….

"Imagine what the emperor demanded of me!" he continued, his voice growing stronger by the second, his eyes shining brightly as he clutched the stone. "Even in his eternal paradise, he still had the drive to conquer, to rule. He thought he would be happy there, content. Alas, not so. I had to build new lands, new kingdoms just so he could prove a conquest. Despite all my efforts, he never forgave me for leaving some of his possessions behind—for that is how he saw them, even people. But a clever chap like me finds whatever loopholes he can, especially when the alternative is to face an angry emperor for the rest of one's life!"

Serves you right, thought Libby. But she didn't dare say so, not with him sitting there with the moonstone in his hands and the fate of Uncle Frank and her friends hanging in the balance. But it nudged the bitterness inside. She clamped her mouth tight, willing herself to hold her tongue.

"The short answer is," continued the Wizard, so caught up in his own story that he took no notice of Libby's dark expression, "I found ways to visit other planes, other dimensions. I even found ways to contact people in this world. It was my only escape. But my mortal body could never return to its mortal home. Think of it, child." He sighed, throwing a plaintive glance her way. "I have no friends, no family, no home. I have my mind, that is true, but I have seen and done such things that I long to be at peace."

Libby fought the impulse to roll her eyes. She glared at the moonstone in his hands instead, and as she did, she saw with absolute certainty that the stone's glow was indeed going *into* the Wizard; she could see it seeping into his skin, then flicking through his veins, like ink spilled through water.

"It is a selfish thing I have done, no doubt about it," he offered, perhaps finally understanding Libby's struggle. His mouth twisted into a wry smile. "I knew you were the solution long ago, Liberty Frye. How can I explain? I saw you in the stars, I suppose you could say. I have had thousands of years to plan for this particular moment. Since my banishment, every string I've tugged, every visit I've made … they have all been orchestrated with you in mind.

"Ine, for example, was set into motion long ago. The first time, she came to me on her own. She sought me out! Well, I suppose I am rather famous … but I digress."

Libby felt the sudden urge to squeeze her head between her hands. Her knees wobbled like tapioca pudding, so she gripped the railing tighter instead, afraid that if she let go, she wouldn't be able to stand. "Um … the *first* time?"

"I mean that, decades before you ever came into the picture—at least in the flesh—your friend conveniently heard of me from the whisperings of the villagers. Well, I may have nudged her curiosity by visiting her much as I first did you, but at the end of the day, it was her choice. Clever girl, that one. She slipped away from home and procured herself four guides to take her up the mountainside! She met me the same way as did you, except that the first time, it was I who gave her the purple berry. Everything else played out the same: I sent her away and she … well, you shall find out soon enough, child. The point is, when you bent time and met her, I tried to give her a fighting chance, but her nature simply won't change. So she followed you to me, where the same fate awaited her. It is senseless, as she has already served her purpose, but what can a Wizard do?"

Libby's brain spun so dizzily that she couldn't even form a question before the Wizard continued:

"And when I met your Uncle Frank all those years ago, my sole intent at *that* time was to simply set things in motion—just like I did with Ine. I had no expectation of getting my hands on the stone *then*, not to mention the fact that I needed its original form rather than three fractured pieces! No, that would take a very special person … *one worth waiting for*. But I shouldn't grow too pleased just yet."

Something about the way he said that cleared the muddle in her mind. "What do you mean by *just yet?*"

The Wizard returned her gaze but said nothing. In the dark, she could see the stone's blue light traveling through his veins, lighting up his arms, his neck, his face, quick and smooth as mercury. The glow coiled through his eyes, growing stronger by the second, and then, even as she stood there, the light burst through the Wizard's pupils, bright and sharp as laser beams.

"Why don't I show you?"

24

Terracotta Warriors

A great roar filled the chamber. Libby stumbled on the ship deck, turning from the Wizard to the pedestal before them, noticing that the water surrounding them must have receded during their visit. One by one, the stairs leading up to the pedestal crumpled into the water below, like collapsing skyscrapers in slow motion, followed by the pedestal. In their place, a whirlpool swirled round and round.

Libby glanced back at the Wizard where he stood on the deck, facing the whirlpool. Light cracked from his eyes, tangling with the air and water, and it felt as if it latched to things invisible therein.

The whirlpool grew wider, stretching its rings through the water, inching nearer the ship. Howling, gurgling sounds rose from its center, and a wind rose with it, lashing against the boat and its mast and the Wizard and Libby. She gripped the deck railing, her limbs quivering and her hair flying every which way so she could barely see, but she could feel it. Something was coming out of her, *pulled* from her. All around the blue light from the Wizard's eyes spun like a cocoon.

"What's happening?"

BAM!

The whirlpool's outer ring hit the ship, then dragged it inside. Down they went, down a spinning, watery hole. Everything fell into silence. There was nothing.

But in the next moment, Libby found she was breathing again. She sputtered, pushing wet strands of hair from her eyes as she glanced frantically about.

"If I had asked," said the Wizard, his voice sounding strange in the darkness, "would you have taken it?"

"Taken what?" Libby choked, blinking into the gloom.

"The stone," said the Wizard.

"I already have," replied another voice.

And before Libby could figure out who had just spoken, white lights flashed overhead, filling the space with such brightness that for a moment she couldn't see a thing. She searched with her hands for something to hold on to, when she realized she must have fallen off the boat. Her palms pressed against something hard, but it felt more like the walls of the tomb. She looked up. Her eyes focused. And then ….

Enormous metal braces arched far over her head, like the supports of a giant tent, only these were intricate—almost like lattice work—and curved down in a perfect semi-circle to meet some sort of platform or walkway above her. The white lights shone from these metal braces, their brightness washing out what lay beyond, but Libby got the impression a roof or canvas must stretch on top of it all.

Was she in a building? A warehouse?

Her head tilted down from the metal braces, her eyes taking in every detail. The walkway she'd first noticed wrapped around the entire space in which she stood, maybe eight or more feet above her, and she noticed the dark gleam of something lining the walls along the walkway. Was it glass? Were those actually modern windows?

Slowly, the significance of her surroundings sank in.

"We aren't in the 1800s anymore!" she whispered.

And Uncle Frank? Ginny? Sal? Buttercup and Esmerelda?

An invisible fist gripped her stomach, twisting and tugging, as her eyes moved in slow motion. They kept going down, leaving the walkway and settling on the space at eye-level. Here, the area in which she stood was very different than that above her. Here, everything was of one hue, like the color of flower pots: the thick, earthen walls around and the packed ground below and something right next to her that was far too close. She stepped away—only to stumble into something else behind her.

"Whoa!" Libby blinked, not quite trusting her vision, but the thing was still there. She found herself face to face with a life-sized clay soldier: a full mouth, wide eyes, long hair coiled into a knot on top of his head, a neat tunic cinched by a belt around his waist. He looked so *real*.

And then she saw another, just inches away, this one wearing what appeared to be a vest with studs over his tunic. The fingers of his left, outstretched hand were curled around some invisible weapon long disintegrated to dust. And behind that soldier she saw another. And another and another. Rows of them, she realized. She stood in an excavated pit between rows of Terracotta Warriors!

I'm in the museum!

"Libby, over here!"

The sound ripped at her nerves. She looked up to see Ginny running over the platform overhead, desperately searching for a way to get down into the pit. And now Libby could see Uncle Frank in his mobile unit, shouting something at Sal who was pulling something with Esmerelda who was yelling something back, all of them way above her on the walkway that circled the room.

Honk!

Buttercup practically smashed into her face, his wings flapping frantically, tangling with her wet hair. Libby sobbed and grabbed him to her, shouting "We're all here! It really worked!" up to the walkway, where everyone else remained. Ginny was shouting excitedly back:

"I can't believe it! We-we were starting to think we'd landed in the wrong place when all of a sudden these blue lights flashed from the ground, like a weird electric storm, and then everything went black and it felt like we were sliding down a slide ... and then this! I can't even—you'd just have had to be there to understand!"

"That's incredible!"

"I know! And all you had to do was wait here for us to show up!"

Libby could only laugh in reply, feeling more relieved than she could ever remember feeling. But then just as abruptly, the reality of her situation hit her: *What about her mother?* It had all happened so fast; the Wizard had never told her, never asked. She'd thought she'd have a *choice.* She'd thought she could send everyone else back while staying behind ....

"Drat," said the Wizard.

Libby spun around. Now that her vision had adjusted to the light, she saw that the Chinese ship had landed in the museum's excavation site, too. It sat several feet behind where she stood, neatly tucked between earthen walls at the bow and stern, and on the deck stood the Wizard, scowling at the earthen wall before him. Stranger still, Libby noticed that the moonstone was conspicuously missing from his grasp, which only needled the worry inside. Where it had gone? She still needed the portal ....

"I was beginning to hope it might go the other way," he continued to grouse, but he wasn't looking at her.

"What—what other way?" called Libby, feeling increasingly panicked. She searched for a route onto the ship deck, but there were no steps, no ladder, and the deck towered several feet above her, making it impossible to climb up. Her eyes darted from left to right, then to the thick walls at the bow and stern, searching for any way to reach to him. She had to get the moonstone and send herself back.

"I did intend to hand it over. I truly did. But … oh, the thrill of feeling so alive! To have that as a *choice* when staring into one's abyss!"

Libby shook her head. She didn't have time for his ramblings; she needed to get that stone.

"I present a new choice."

The sound of those words sizzled in the air. Who had just spoken? Not the Wizard. Not her. Definitely not Uncle Frank or her friends far above….

Slowly, ever so slowly, she turned in the direction of the Wizard's gaze.

Have you ever seen a witch? Not the ordinary-looking-person-with-secret-extraordinary-powers-like-Libby kind of witch, but an actual, that's-all-there-is-folks witch? The kind you might dress up as on Halloween; the kind of witch you might dream about on dark, stormy nights? The kind whose face shows both resignation and single-minded resolve, for that person has spent an entire lifetime devoted to a solitary goal, so devoted that everything else that once made up who they were, or that showed a glimmer of who they might become, has been pressed and squeezed away hour by hour, day by day, year by year, until there is only that one thing left?

Libby had seen such a witch before, and she'd seen that witch again, just a few nights ago, without ever suspecting it. How could she have possibly suspected such an impossible thing?

And yet ….

An old woman stepped from behind a partition and stood on top of the earthen wall by the ship's bow. She wore a long robe with a shawl thrown over her head, covering most of her face. And in her hands … she held the moonstone.

"That's the lady from the harbor again!" Ginny exclaimed from above. "The one who gave us the clothes and then showed up with Liesel Herrmann later!"

And while Libby didn't know who Liesel Herrmann was or what Ginny meant by showing up later, she did know that the old woman before her wasn't just the harbor-shore woman. No, that woman was someone *more*. Because most of all, for the very first time, Libby also recognized her voice.

"You're—"

The woman turned her head, causing the shawl to slip off her hair and settle around her shoulders. And even though Libby had, seconds before, finally realized who she was, the sight of her face sent shock waves through her.

"Sabine?" whispered Libby.

"Ine," sighed the Wizard, sounding wearier than even before when he'd suffered his coughing fits. "When will you finally learn?"

25

HOSTAGE

Libby's ears rang. She opened her mouth to speak, but nothing would come out. It took several seconds to realize Sabine had turned and was now speaking to her.

"I want to go back," Sabine was saying, still clutching the moonstone in her hands. Libby noticed the stone glowed a faint blue, but there was no sign of its powers transferring *into* Sabine the way it had for the Wizard. Sabine's voice shook. "I … I have waited so long for this moment. It is because of you that I was sent away in the first place. This is your chance to make it right, Liberty Frye. Send me back!"

Libby blinked. Then she swallowed. Above her, she heard Uncle Frank's and Sal's and Ginny's shouts. Below her, Buttercup honked and waddled around her legs, as if guarding her from Sabine's dreadful gaze. She turned from Sabine to the Wizard, her mind in a complete fog.

The Wizard grunted. "Ine, dear girl, don't you see? It won't work. You can't undo what has already been done!"

"What's been done?"

"But there must be a way!" cried Sabine, ignoring Libby's question. She shook the stone in her gnarled hands. "She channels its power, does she not? I just saw you use it, *use her!* I have been waiting here for hours on end; and before that, years and years of planning. A lifetime; an unnatural, miserable lifetime!"

He turned to Libby. "Child, tell her for yourself. Did you not witness her very form, just days ago on the shores of Qingdao? And did it do anything to get rid of your presence before her younger self decided to accompany you? Did it prevent her terrible fate that day on the mountain?"

Libby gulped down what felt like a goose egg in her throat, and even as she opened her mouth to reply, she couldn't quite believe what she was about to ask: "Are … are you saying that Sabine … that Sabine is actually *Ine?*"

"Why else would I be in this place?" snapped the old woman. "But I do not know of what nonsense this vile man speaks of! If I were to have already gone back, I wouldn't be here now!"

"B-but you were there, just like the Wizard says!" blubbered Libby. "You were the lady who gave us the clothes! How could that be you … and you be Ine, both at the same time?"

But the question hit her like a slap. Memories of their

arrival in Qingdao flashed through her mind; of chasing Ine through those streets; of that feeling of déjà vu; of the mysterious bite marks; of what the Wizard had said about perception; of what both he and Xue had mentioned about bending time ....

"She doesn't know!" shouted Uncle Frank. "Phenomenal! It-it's a closed time-like curve!"

And in his excitement, he must have hit one of the buttons on his mobile unit, because the hover vent erupted into life, practically flinging Uncle Frank out of his chair as it shot into the air.

"He is on to the general idea," replied the Wizard, regarding Sabine. "There was a fifty-fifty chance, more or less, that a different outcome could take place, and small variations may occur that don't affect the final result, but once it's done, the conclusion remains! You'll just keep repeating yourself!"

"What's a closed time ... whatever it is?" interjected Libby. She turned to Uncle Frank, who had just landed beside her in the pit, and even in her stunned state, she couldn't help but notice his enthusiasm. His eyes glittered and danced—he looked like a kid on Christmas morning—which seemed deeply inappropriate under the circumstances.

"You bent time on your birthday, kiddo, right?" he explained, speaking so fast that it was hard for Libby to keep up. "And in going back in time to 1871 and meeting a young Sabine when we arrived in Qingdao, you created a loop: a closed time-like curve! But ... but no!" He continued, now waggling a finger in the air as his eyes darted wildly about.

"No, this is fantastic! Is … is it possible that you are *right now,* even as we are here, creating the loop?" If Uncle Frank had been standing, he would have collapsed on the floor, he was that overcome. His eyes darted from Libby to the Wizard. "You must have already sent Ine on this journey at least once before! Before Libby ever encountered her in Qingdao … am I correct?"

"You are not *wrong,*" said the Wizard.

"So the young Sabine," continued Uncle Frank, practically tripping over his words, "that is to say, Ine—was teleported by the Wizard to another place, where she grew up, determined to find a way to return to her past to correct the mistake! But the grown Ine—that is to say, Sabine—can't interfere with her younger self, so the best she can do is to try to change the course of events before you and Ine meet! That's why she brought you the clothes! She was trying to get you to go away before you ever met her younger self! But she isn't successful in that attempt, thus creating the loop which brings her back here!"

"This is my *life,* old man!" snarled Sabine, her mouth twisting with bitterness. "You speak as if it is some sort of science project! Do you know what it's like?" she continued, staring straight at Libby with those awful, ghostly grey eyes— the same grey Libby remembered when she'd first met Sabine in Germany—and it struck her that this woman she remembered as the Witch in the Woods, Sabine-turned-Ine- turned-Sabine, really could be the same person; Libby could *feel* it, feel all that sorrow and resentment and loneliness that had dragged at Sabine's years, bleaching away any joy just as it had bleached away any trace of blue from her eyes ....

"I was a mere child—younger than you are now!" Sabine continued miserably. "You told me such things as to captivate my interest, then took me with you to visit this *Wizard* you spoke so highly of, and through your energy—energy this man used and *still* uses—I was sent to the other side of the world! And that wretched purple berry proved my only token of what sent me there!"

"It is cruel what I did," admitted the Wizard. "What can I say? It is in my nature to experiment. I simply can't help it, but really, Ine my dear, you cannot blame Liberty Frye for your choices—"

"My choices?" spat Sabine. "I had no choice!"

The Wizard tutted and shook his head. "I am afraid that simply is not the case. You see, Frank is quite right: you first came to me on your own. You just do not remember because now, the past has been altered by Liberty Frye's visit on the shores of Qingdao. I tried to give you a chance, but you still chose to come to me. It is indeed a pity, because all I needed you for in first place was to set things in motion, which you'd already done beautifully, by the way—"

"Wait a minute!" yelled Libby, raising her hands and squeezing the sides of her temples. "So ...," she resumed, doing her best to break things down into digestible pieces, but it felt as if the facts floated around her like bits of dried leaves in water, slipping away from her grasp at each attempt. "So ... for me—for everyone else here, in fact—Ine was sent away yesterday afternoon, right before the Wizard sent *me* through a portal to Xi'an, right?"

"From your perspective, child, that is correct," the Wizard agreed pleasantly.

"But from Ine's perspective," persisted Libby, determined to see the thought through, "since she wasn't part of *our* time travel, these *same events* that happened yesterday for me, happened years and years ago for her, right? Like, over a hundred years ago! But ... that's impossible!"

"Just tell me *why!*" moaned Sabine. Tears leaked down her cheeks as she turned to the Wizard. Even as venom blazed across her face, she too had a look of desperation, of pleading, like a child longing to understand. "I've thought about it over and over; I remember every moment of that day. It was *you* who mentioned the tomb and how Liberty Frye would be visiting it shortly. It is how I knew to wait here; I calculated everything— using stars and trees and books!"

"I was counting on that," murmured the Wizard.

"So is that it? Is that why you sent me away? Was I *punished* for my curiosity?"

The Wizard sighed. "No, Ine. For mine."

It felt to Libby as if she heard these words in slow motion, and the awfulness of what the Wizard had done sank into her. She raised her gaze to Ginny, who remained on the platform above, her eyes wide with disbelief.

"You have to understand," the Wizard was saying, regarding Sabine with an expression that almost looked like pity, "it was the ultimate experiment; I gambled with my own fate as much as yours! Even though you have served your purpose, I knew what would happen if you weren't here to stop me today. You saw how, just minutes ago, I lapped up the stone's power in my hands, did you not? You saw the eagerness within, despite my resolve to let it all go. But how could I resist? How could anyone?"

His voice broke, and from where Libby stood below him in the pit, she could hear his breathing: wheezing, rattling gasps.

"If Sabine had not snatched the stone from my hands," he concluded in a rasp, "I fear things might have ended rather differently ... for all of us here."

Libby nodded blearily. Random thoughts popped into her mind, but nothing seemed to tie together. She felt like a fish in a fishbowl, watching the world outside function with different rules, different laws of nature she could not understand. In fact, the only thing she understood for certain was that Uncle Frank and her friends were here with her at the Terracotta Warriors Museum, and that the Wizard and Sabine both wanted the stone.

"And how *might* things end differently?" demanded Sabine, wiping the tears from her face with the hem of her shawl. "I know how they ended for *me*. Would you like to hear of it?" She glared down at Libby. "It is such a wonderful tale—it might even surpass those stories in your grandfather's precious book!"

The mention of her grandfather and the Brothers Grimm book seemed like a strange topic considering the present circumstance, and it only served to make Libby feel even more confused.

"Because of *you,*" Sabine hissed the word, as if it were poison flung from her mouth, "I spent years in and out of orphanages. No one believed my story; they were sure I was … *touched.* Each time I ran away, I was found again. By the time I was finally able to leave, I discovered that my family was no longer. My father had perished during a mission trip, my mother from grief. I've endured wars; I've witnessed friends meet their ends from violence as much as old age. I've seen cities built, destroyed, then rebuilt again. None of these hold a candle to the agony of losing my family in such a way."

Libby's head swam; too many questions collided in her brain, and it was with a sense of relief that she heard Ginny shout:

"But Ine was a kid back in 1871, right? So you can't possibly be her, even if you are a witch!"

Sabine turned impatiently to the walkway encircling the excavation pit.

"Ginny, is it?" she pursed her withered lips. "Yes, I remember. Well if you recall, the fruit of Barvultmir happens to have some potent powers. Extending life is one of them. Liberty Frye," she continued, turning her attention back to where Libby stood in the pit below, "did you not witness how those purple berries revived your parents from Zelna's spell? Or how your mother grinds the fruit into various tinctures for your Uncle Frank? Or indeed, how she uses them on herself to fight for the life you take from her?"

Libby sucked in a sharp breath. Sabine's words stung her to the quick, but she shook her head and tried to focus.

"I see you are beginning to *catch on,*" Sabine pulled her shawl snugly about her shoulders. "As for me, it did not take long to notice how the fruit of Barvultmir delayed the signs of time upon my appearance. And so, when I first met your Aunt Zelna when she was young—perhaps around your age—I myself appeared to be a girl of only thirteen or so."

Could this really be true? Libby pressed her fingers to her eyes, trying to still the pounding behind them. She tried to remember all Sabine had told her before, when she'd first met her in that cottage in the woods. It felt like a lifetime ago, even though it had been less than a year ….

"But what about the Devil's Cave?" she recalled, grasping at random memories. "You helped me. Why? I mean, if you really are Ine, then why did you help me *then* if you blame me for what happened to you? Why didn't you say anything?"

"Because all of life is a flick of dominos, child," the Wizard opined in a weary voice. "Just as I've used Ine for my own means, so it is that Sabine has used you. One little choice sets off a chain reaction that forms reality as we know it. For example, had Ine never been sent away by me, she would never have searched for a means to return home. She would never have devoted her life to the study of magic, never learned to read the stars, never listened to the whisperings of trees."

"But when I met her last year in Germany—"

"Your memory of that occasion," interrupted the Wizard, "is different than Sabine's memory of these same events. When you met her last year, it was *before* you bent time. All she knew of you *then* was what she'd seen in the stars and what she'd heard from the trees … things she'd discovered long before you met her; before your mother even knew you were in her womb."

"What …," whispered Libby, staring back up at the Wizard, "did she discover?"

"Your powers, of course," said the Wizard. "It is why I sent Ine away in the first place; she was the first piece of my puzzle. I needed *her* to need *you!*" He sighed as he lifted a pale hand. The blue glow that had once coursed through his veins was gone, and whatever energy he had gathered from the moonstone was obviously entirely expended, for he looked so feeble and colorless that he appeared more like a ghost than a living person. "Well, it could have been anyone, I suppose, but when you live for thousands of years, any curious pawn that fits the bill will do, and the matter of a hundred years or so is nothing but the blink of an eye. So, Ine it was."

For a moment, no one said anything. And then:

"*I* was a mere *piece of your puzzle?*" Sabine's voice quivered with rage. "My whole life—everything I have suffered—is simply because I would *do?*"

"*Someone* had to," returned the Wizard, utterly unfazed. He turned his attention back to Libby. "It all goes back to what I was saying earlier: If Sabine had never discovered your potential, she wouldn't have seen you as her one hope of returning to her past. As such, she wouldn't have protected you by warning your mother to flee from her homeland before you were born. If Gretchen hadn't fled, then you would have been destroyed by Zelna when you were a baby—that was Zelna's original plan, after all …."

"I saw you in the stars," moaned Sabine. "That is all I can say! I know you can help me!"

"And if you had never been lured from the safety of your home in Mississippi," continued the Wizard, insensible to Sabine's tears, "you would never have met Sabine and learned of your powers. If Sabine had not come to your aid, you would never have defeated Zelna in the cave, never realized the extent of your ability ... or absorbed Zelna's energy for yourself. Was it not the unwitting harnessing of her energy, combined with yours, that sent you back in time? Was it not this very condition that set you on your quest for me? Was it not me who has now brought you to Sabine, complete with the moonstone?"

For a moment, Libby forgot to breathe.

Sabine glowered at them all, a terrible mix of confusion and hatred flashing from her eyes.

"Did it not take all of this to show you who you really are?" concluded the Wizard in a whisper. "To make you desperate for a solution, an answer, a way out from the horror within?"

Libby stood, transfixed. She had no answer. Images of her mother flickered through her mind. Of her hair growing whiter and whiter. Of the flash of those brilliant violet eyes, once so full of life, growing dimmer by the day ....

"It is time for *my* question now," hissed Sabine, and the coldness in her voice rattled through the air as she held the moonstone before her. "Are you desperate *enough*, Liberty Frye?"

26

THE SPACE BETWEEN

Libby felt Uncle Frank's hand close protectively around her arm. And from above her, she heard Ginny shout:

"You think just because you have a stupid stone, you can bully Libby like that? She's a witch now! She can … do stuff."

Libby cringed.

"Show her, Libby!"

Libby shuffled her feet as she peeked up at Sabine, feeling decidedly awkward. She racked her brain for a spell, an idea, *anything* she could do, but nothing came to mind other than the fervent wish that Ginny wouldn't say things like that ….

"She's the most powerful witch in *the whole world!*" Ginny expounded, and with each word, Libby felt herself shrinking more and more. "I mean, technically, I don't think there's ever been a contest or anything, but if there was one, she'd totally win! Libby, you've got to show her! You know, that *thing!*"

But Libby had no idea what *thing* Ginny referred to; she doubted very much if Ginny knew. She mentally ran through every spell in her spell book, but there was nothing in there to handle repercussions of time travel gone awry, stolen magical amulets or unfortunate encounters between wizards and rote witches ....

"That's exactly what I am requesting," replied Sabine. "Yes, show me, Liberty Frye. Show me how to return to my past. Do this, and the stone is yours."

"But why does she even *need* the stone?" demanded Ginny. "We're already back in our own time!"

Libby felt Uncle Frank's fingers twitch against her arm, as if Ginny's words had struck a nerve he hadn't quite known was there until that moment.

Sabine turned to regard Libby.

"It is true you are returned to your eleventh birthday," she said, and it seemed to Libby as if she took pleasure in this particular moment, as if she had waited *so very long* to drop this information at her feet. "Though it is night here, in Biloxi, it is only a little after ten in the morning, on the day when your powers are strongest, when your stars align ...."

Understanding settled into Uncle Frank's eyes.

"Why didn't I think of it before?" he muttered, and despite having no idea what he was talking about, Libby felt prickles of alarm creep up her neck.

"Think of *what* before?"

He swiveled to face Libby directly and grabbed her by the shoulders, his expression taking on that frantic, distracted look he always had while working out an especially convoluted problem. "We traveled back to the 1800s, to a time before you and I existed ... until we did. Right?"

"Um ... right?"

"So right there, we've taken our universe out of itself. We've put ourselves into a time before we existed, thus creating a new reality where we exist in that time! And now, the Wizard must have used *your* power to bring us from the 1800s back to modern-day China on your birthday, but in our time— that is, our lives back home—we were most likely on our boat, leaving the Biloxi marina at this moment!"

"What?"

"It would seem," continued Uncle Frank, speaking even faster than before, "we've got parallel universes of us existing at the same time: the 'us' *here* and the 'us' sailing away from the marina!"

"It is a conundrum, to be sure," remarked the Wizard.

"Even if we return through the wormhole you created on your birthday, we've already created two versions of ourselves! What happens to the space in between *now* and when the wormhole was created? What happens to those we left in the other one? What happens to us? How can there be a present when the past is missing? How can two versions of us exist in the same place?"

The Wizard shrugged. "It *would* be fascinating to find out."

"Enough of your experiments!" snapped Libby. She

pushed away the wet hairs sticking to her forehead and turned to Uncle Frank, determined to keep her voice steady. "I'm not following half of this, but I think I get the most important part. Basically, we were supposed to return to modern times at the exact time we first left … which didn't happen. Right?"

"Quite honestly, there is more at stake than simply making your loop," the Wizard mused. "Good thing I've created your portal. I simply can't see another way to fix this predicament if you don't use the moonstone. Everything your Uncle Frank just said would hold true … if it weren't for the fact that we are here … and not here at the same time. Consider our current state of being a sort of bubble, suspended just at the mouth of the wormhole you originally created." He broke into a sudden fit of coughing before resuming hoarsely: "It takes some doing to keep it stable—if it collapses before you've traveled through, I'm afraid that's the end for all of you—and it is your one chance to return to your own time while sending Sabine back to hers. Well, it's a nifty trick; one of the perks of Wizardry I suppose …."

Sabine raised the amulet high in her hands, as if brandishing the greatest prize in all the world.

"If you love these people as much as you *say* you do, then you must use the portal. You *need* the portal. Send me back, child, and it is yours. Come now; there is little time to waste!"

Libby pressed her hands against her eyes, for it suddenly felt as if her brain might burst through them, and she was so bamboozled by the Wizard and Sabine and the moonstone and the portal and all the gibberish about their time-traveling predicament that pressing her eyes seemed like the most sensible thing to do at the moment. But Sabine's words echoed in her mind. *Little time to waste.* Hadn't Ine just said that exact same thing, just days before? The throbbing behind her eyes expanded into her ears, pounding and pounding, so she felt as if she were swimming underwater and running out of air, but the surface was too far above her to reach …

"Eight minutes," the Wizard wheezed. "I am dying, after all. There is only so long I can keep this up."

… and she remembered what the Wizard had said to her before, when she'd floated in that inky darkness, right after Ine had been sent through the portal: he'd said she was the co-creator of her reality, hadn't he? What happened next … it was at least partly up to her.

"But this is ridiculous!" huffed Ginny. "How is she supposed to send Sabine back?"

"How indeed?" rasped the Wizard. "Can you *imagine* it, child? Can you see a way?"

Libby dropped her hands. Her eyes locked on Sabine, even as the Wizard's words squeezed through her mind, snaking between the booming in her ears, the pounding in her heart, the throbbing in her temples that grew so strong it felt as if her forehead might shatter from the pressure inside.

Could she imagine it?

Perception and energy. Magic. It flowed through her; she felt it a part of her; she a part of it. She was a part of everything. Everything was part of everything. *Everything:* every hair and blood cell and raindrop and heartbeat, all love and starlight and thought and ... time. All of it was connected in ways invisible to the eye, but not to perception.

But to perceive, she had to first imagine ....

Sabine remained standing on the earthen wall. Libby remained below in the pit. But the space between them became no more than the space between her own layers of skin. And the memories of that foggy night on the shores of Qingdao were as real, were as *present,* as the Warriors surrounding them.

"Okay, Sabine," she whispered. "Let's go."

They were bathed in light. The moonstone glowed inside Sabine's hands, radiating like a thousand suns, a tunnel of white light flowing from its heart straight into Libby. She raised her arms and felt it, felt its power, and she was dizzy from its touch. She felt as if it burned away everything that formed her body, but the burn did not hurt; no, it felt as if she had wings and could fly, with no form to hold her down, and she could soar and soar into skies and beyond: into galaxies, into universes, into ... everything.

And she heard Sabine sobbing. She felt all her joys and sorrows and love and hate and hope and despair ... it flowed between and through them like a current. She felt Sabine's tears, too, and knew she shared them as well; it was almost too much to bear.

And then ...

Libby imagined. She pulled at the light flowing through her, and the more she held it the stronger it grew until its tail became a blaze that stretched across all time. She exhaled in astonishment as she peered into Sabine's ghostly eyes, witnessing flashes of her long, lonely life. She saw Ine sitting on a cot in an orphanage, once again a little girl, skinny legs drawn up against her chest, rocking back and forth, whispering frantically over and over again:

Mama, Papa, I will find you. I promise. I will find a way to come back ....

And then, Ine was now older, perhaps the same age as Libby. She stood in a forest clearing, a ragged coat hanging over thin shoulders and a secondhand suitcase by her feet. She looked around, those pale eyes already more grey than blue. What did she see? Libby peered into her mind, parting the waves of light to see closer:

Ine stood in that clearing, staring at a stone tower and a squat, stone hut with a wooden door. *Home.* Those were the words floating in her mind. She formed them into a whisper. *Welcome home*, Ine murmured to herself, and then grabbed her suitcase and stepped toward the wooden door. The light all around began to fade; this stage was ending. But Libby lingered there for a moment longer; there was something she needed to see. But what? She peered closer into the light, straining to see a last glimpse of Ine's world in that moment. The wooden door was closing. Ine faced an empty, barren room. Cobwebs and mildew. Years of disuse. A stone fireplace so in neglect that even the firewood had long turned to dust. A gleam of light twinkled through the closing door. Ine heaved a sigh, then grabbed a stick from the ground and jammed it under the door, keeping it open so she could see enough to clean. She squinted once more into the sunlight … and then Libby saw it:

Just beyond the stone tower, where the woods tangled around the clearing in a wall of bark and leaves and moss, stood a tree singular from the rest. Bright red. Purple berries. *Barvultmir.*

The scene dissolved. Years passed. So many years. Days and nights of endless solitude. Books and maps, charts and notepads filled Ine's living room. But where was Ine? The door stood slightly ajar, the cool air of an autumn evening wafting into the hut. The door creaked open from the breeze, revealing the clearing outside where Ine, now a young woman, lay on the ground with her spyglass, searching the starry sky ….

More years came and went. And yet, Sabine barely appeared to have aged. She stood in a cobblestone square beside a large bronze statue. She looked so pretty, her hair twisted up in a loose bun, her shoes, though well-worn, polished to a sparkle. Her palms pressed against the skirt of her dress with its purple and green pattern of violets and vines. She'd made it just for the occasion, staying up for nights on end as she cut and stitched. But what was the occasion? And then Libby saw:

A handsome man walked toward Ine. Tall. Thin. Warm, dark eyes that, when they met Ine's, felt like liquid. Ine's heart fluttered. Her palms grew sweaty. She tried to compose herself and look casual. She cleared her throat and smiled.

"Hello, Klaus," she said.

But then her smile grew bitter, forming needles that clawed at her heart. Klaus was speaking of a beautiful girl named Giselle. He was engaged! He looked so happy and yet ... bewildered. As if he were not sure of his own good fortune. Or perhaps it wasn't that. Perhaps, even then, he wondered ....

Sabine blinked back tears. She forced a smile though her throat ached as if it had turned to glass. She mumbled something, and then her pretty dress and polished shoes and whimsical, delicate hair were walking away from the statue. She walked and walked without looking back, but Libby could hear sobs erupting from her. And then panting as Sabine ran from the town, now through the trees until, once again, she faced a stone tower and a stone hut and a tree. Once more, all alone.

No friends.

No family.

Another scene. Two years later. Klaus stood at the door of her hut, his posture hunched so he could step through the squat doorway. But once inside, she saw he still stooped. And his face and skin looked as if they'd aged years beyond him. That warmth in his eyes was gone. He held out a book in his hand: a beautiful green, leather-bound book. The Brothers Grimm collection of fairy tales. Could she help him? He needed a rune ....

Sabine swallowed all the bitterness and tears. All the resentment. Of course she would, she smiled. Her smile felt like ice in her chest, but on the outside, it appeared warm enough. She did her work, and then he was gone.

But wait ....

Libby lingered there. She saw an hour pass, then two,

Sabine pacing beside the fireplace, her eyes darting to and fro, as if impatiently waiting ....

"Ah!"

Sabine ran to her table, flinging away seeds and twigs and freeze-dried fungus and crushed snail shells and a tin of peppered worm gizzard and who knows what else, now grabbing a feather that had been sharpened to a point and dipping the point into a yellow-hued liquid. She held the feather over a sheet of blank paper. She took a deep breath.

"So there you are, Klaus," she murmured.

Her eyes rolled up so that only her whites gleamed through open lids. She began to mutter and moan as if in a trance. What was she seeing?

Her hand twitched, and then, as if it were connected to another thought, another brain, another being outside of Sabine, it began to write. Faster and faster, it scribbled letters that turned into words that formed sentences. And then, just as quickly, it stopped.

Sabine's eyes returned to normal. With shaking hands, she lifted the paper from the table and carried it with her to the hearth. She sat in a chair covered with some sort of vegetable matter and lifted the page so it was illuminated by the fire.

Letters appeared over the page, curling like smoke into words that glowed eerily in the light. What did they say? Sabine scanned the page, bitterness once more settling over her features. But before Libby could see what Sabine read, the scene once more faded.

The years continued. Sabine, who had stayed impossibly

young for so long, now appeared as an old woman. Once more, she stood in the clearing by her hut, only now the tree that had shaded her hallowed space was nothing but a blackened stump. Sabine flung her coat over her shoulders and walked toward town. Where she went, Libby wasn't sure, but the next thing she saw was Sabine boarding a train. And then Sabine was in a city, walking up the steps to a bank. And then Sabine was giving a code to a bank official who was escorting her to a dark room with rows of padlocked boxes. And then Sabine had money. Lots and lots of money.

More time went by. How much? She saw a girl opening the door to Sabine's hut. It was dark out and the girl was frightened. Libby sucked in a sharp breath. It was her! She was the girl! It was the night she'd first met Sabine! She saw the fireplace, the old white dog, the books scattered about the floor, the dried frog legs hanging from the rafters .... And then she was gone. But Sabine remained in her hut, now seated at her table. A small spell book was open before her—*Das Klein Buch der Magie*—and it was turned to the back page. Sabine was writing something across that last, empty sheet, something in an ink that remained invisible. Suddenly, Sabine froze. She turned around, her hideous face staring straight at Libby.

Libby gasped.

Immediately, the visions vanished and Libby stood once more in the pit, facing Sabine, who stood on the earthen wall above. Only now Sabine was encircled by the light so she seemed *a part of it*, her form becoming less and less, as if she were dissolving. She smiled.

CHAPTER 26

"So you see," Sabine whispered.

And then ….

She was gone.

27

İNTO ᴛHE LIGHT

he moonstone dropped through empty space. To Libby, it was as if everything in the museum stood still except the fall of the amulet. No sound. No movement. No breath. She felt as if she'd been kicked in the stomach. She found herself doubled over, struggling for air, her eyes locked on the moonstone.

"Once the portal is used," the Wizard rasped from above, "it will be no more."

She forced herself to a standing position and ran to catch the stone. Its glow burned brighter upon contact, as if responding to her touch. She glanced up at the Wizard, and she saw that he had shifted his position, so that he stood on the wall facing the ship, at the exact spot Sabine had been moments before, and more than that, Libby noticed that he was now nothing but a whisper of a man, as though he were disintegrating before her eyes.

"It is just as well," he continued feebly. "I will say goodbye to this world, but the rest remains up to you. Will you embrace it? Or will you hide from it?"

"But my mom …."

"Even now?" asked the Wizard. "Before, you did not understand the power you held. Now, your eyes are opened."

"But I don't see a way—"

"Perhaps because you haven't imagined one yet …." His voice broke as he fell into another fit of coughing, his lungs rattling like an empty tin can with a rusty nail. And then:

"Three minutes, Liberty Frye."

His countdown seemed to break some sort of spell. Uncle Frank shuffled in his mobile unit, Buttercup honked and waddled at Libby's feet, and a great clanging came from overhead. Libby turned to see Ginny and Esmerelda and Sal running through a gate that had just opened, now down the stairs, now into the pit where she stood with the amulet.

The moonstone glowed brighter, its light circling wider by the second, spinning until it lifted from her hands and hovered in front of the Chinese boat, a blaze of circling blue light swirling around a white-hot center. The portal grew and grew until it stretched at least ten feet in every direction.

Libby turned from the moonstone's portal to Uncle Frank and, when she peered into his face, saw that look once more— the look she had seen that last night on the *Liberté*.

"If you stay here …," he began, as if guessing her thoughts, but then he stopped. "No matter what you do or where you go in life, kiddo, there's always going to be a Zelna."

"You know she's gone, right?"

"That's not what I meant."

Libby glanced from Uncle Frank to the portal, and for a split second, she imagined watching him disappearing through it … and Ginny … and Sal … and Esmerelda … and Buttercup. She imagined the portal sucking them up—gone in that single flash—and then disappearing from her life forever. And what then? Would she live the rest of it like Sabine? Alone, with nothing but her memories? And that loneliness eating at her heart like a worm at an apple, rotting it away? And what of her parents? What would Uncle Frank say to them? That she chose to run away?

"Will you help me?" she whispered.

Uncle Frank grabbed her hand with both of his, his long, calloused fingers closing around her palm. "You don't need my help." He looked straight into her eyes, and the warmth in his own told her without a doubt that his words were true. "You just need to believe in your own ability."

"But …," she heard herself say, "I'm so scared!"

"We're all scared of something, kiddo. If you focus on that, it becomes all you see."

"Sixty seconds, Liberty Frye."

She could barely hear the Wizard's voice, and when she glanced up, the blazing swirl of light hid him entirely from view. She looked back at Uncle Frank, then to Ginny, who stood with one hand on her hip, brows creased, shouting impatiently as she jabbed an index finger toward the swirling portal ....

Libby almost laughed out loud.

She had a *choice*. And just like that night, nearly a year ago on the Solstice of Aramaar, she saw that her mind was her own—no one else's—and it was up to her to be its master, to *be* and to *become* whatever it was she believed in.

"Libby!" Ginny bellowed. "We've got to go! Now!"

Libby exhaled and squeezed Uncle Frank's hand. Tears welled in her eyes, but she didn't let go to wipe them away. Instead, she reached out to Ginny with her other hand, just as Esmerelda scooped up Buttercup and Sal stood by their side.

"It's about time!" snapped Ginny, glaring at her best friend. "What are we waiting for?"

Libby half snorted, half laughed through her tears. "This," she said.

And then together, they entered the light.

❀

The glow was still there, but it had grown hazy. Strange glints shifted and shimmered around her. It was difficult to see, but as her eyes adjusted, Libby could make out the familiar spire of the stone generator before her, pointing toward the open sky like a sundial.

"Phenomenal, isn't it?" murmured Uncle Frank.

Libby jerked, feeling as if she were waking from a deep sleep and everything moved in slow motion. It took another second to realize Uncle Frank was beside her. Of course he was. Hadn't they entered the portal together? But if so, then where was Ginny?

Uncle Frank turned his attention from the stone and smiled, his warm, dark eyes full of wonder.

"Holy Macaroni!" Ginny's voice warbled somewhere behind them, and the sound flooded Libby with relief. "Did we get sent to Biloxi in that ancient boat?"

"I ... I think so!" Libby managed to reply. It felt so strange to speak in the open air.

She squinted over the shimmering water and spotted the Biloxi pier in the distance, and before them, three other ships sailed peacefully from the bay, just as she remembered. Another ship dotted the horizon, and even from this distance, she could make out the curious shape of the ship's sails—like inverted triangles. All around, the grey sky hovered thick and hot, the sticky breeze smacking against her skin like plastic wrap. *Home.*

"But what kind of boat *is* this?" continued Ginny, now staggering toward them as she held on to the deck railing. "I mean, is it even seaworthy? And ... oh my goodness!" She gaped at the sail. "Is that a *dragon*?"

As if in reply, the ornately-painted sail—decorated with a red dragon against a yellow background and surrounded by puffy blue clouds—billowed from a sudden gust of wind, tugging the ship forward.

"Darn skippy!" called Sal from where he stood beside the mast. "I've headed her back to the marina!"

Ginny glanced from the sail to the ancient wood planks below her feet. Then she nervously scanned the bay.

"So ... how do we know we're back to where we should be? I mean, are we going to encounter our former selves somewhere around here?" Her gaze darted from left to right, but the only other boats to be seen were the three ships already in the bay and the one on their horizon. "What if I just keep my eyes shut?" she continued to ramble, and with each passing syllable her tone grew more and more shrill. "Yeah! That could work! If we don't see our other selves, then it will be like we're not there, right? So ... quick! Let's all close our eyes!"

Uncle Frank chuckled. "I think it's safe to keep your eyes open, Ginny. In fact, I recommend it."

Ginny opened one eye and peered dubiously back at him.

"Look around, kid," Sal said as he scanned the bay. "The *Liberté* is conspicuously missing. If we returned too soon, then she would be right about where we are at this moment. I think the Wizard actually kept his word!"

"It's incredible," marveled Uncle Frank.

Buttercup honked in agreement and flapped in circles above them, followed by Esmerelda's scolding: "Sit-still-you-silly-fowl! After-all-we-have-been-through, we-do-not-need-any-more-excitement!"

Libby shook her head, still not quite believing their good fortune. She stared again at the stone generator before her, and even though the stone maintained its peculiar, octopus-like shape, gone were the blue lights, the glow from within, the humming energy. In fact, looking at the thing now, it seemed laughable that this hunk of contorted—but otherwise unremarkable rock—had been used to bring an entire underground city to life.

"Besides," added Uncle Frank, squinting over the water, "it's Peter and Gretchen we need to be worried about. I wonder what they've witnessed while standing on that pier ...."

Libby lifted her eyes to the marina in the distance. From where she stood, she could now see her parents' figures. They looked so small from here, like little dolls standing on a doll-pier surrounded by doll-boats and more doll-people. But the water stretching between them was real. *They* were real.

Her heart fluttered and jumped. It pounded and skipped. Soon. After so long. And yet ....

What about her mom?

"How do you feel?" demanded Ginny, as if reading her thoughts. Even though Uncle Frank and Sal had reassured her enough to open her eyes, her sense of unease had apparently transferred to another concern ....

"Last time we were here ... I mean, the last time it was your birthday, you were having those waves of nausea, right? Isn't that what you said you felt right before you time-blasted us into the 1800s?" She fidgeted, then let go of the railing with one hand so that she could smooth her ponytail. "So ... not to be rude or anything," she gripped the railing once more with both hands, "but ... er, are you feeling dizzy now?"

Without thinking, Libby raised her hand to her sternum,

where just hours before, her moonstone necklace had been. Nothing was there, of course.

"Anything out of the ordinary?" pressed Ginny, as if half expecting Libby to explode into a cloud of squid ink or something. "Any … *strange* sensations?"

Libby thought about that. She took a deep breath as if reaching somewhere inside. "Maybe a little," she admitted. "But I know what it is now."

Ginny inhaled sharply … or was it a muted sob? Libby wasn't sure.

"So …," Ginny cleared her throat, and when she spoke next, her voice wobbled a little, "can you try to control it?"

Libby glanced from her best friend back to the pier where her parents stood. She had a *choice*.

"No," she said, setting her jaw. "I *will*."

And though it was such a simple thing to say, the weight behind those words settled upon her shoulders. Libby continued looking to the pier in the distance; even with her parents in sight, it was difficult to believe that she really was back in Biloxi, complete with Uncle Frank and her friends. It had all happened in an instant.

How could that be?

Other than their clothes and the unusual Chinese ship, there was no indication that weeks and weeks had passed for all of them while to her parents, a mere moment had passed. Could it be possible that it had never actually happened? That it had all been a dream? That the *Liberté* had never existed and that, in her confused state of mind, she simply didn't remember setting sail from the Biloxi pier on a Chinese ship? That there had never been a rubber ducky or time machine? That they'd never been teleported or held hostage by pirates or met Kai or sailed to China or befriended a young Sabine or voyaged up a mountain or even met the Wizard ....

After all, how could she ever know for sure? The only way she could try to *prove* it was through the differences between now and when she'd first left the pier: Different boat, different clothes, and in lieu of her trusty backpack, she now sported an embroidered satchel around her waist. She probably stank a little, too. So was that what makes something real? If it changes you?

The quickly-approaching pier brought her thoughts back to the present. And those last few seconds felt like a thousand, but finally, the ship glided to a stop, just feet from where Libby's parents stood.

"What-what on earth just *happened?*" sputtered her dad as they clamored off the boat deck and onto the pier. "We were leaving to get picnic supplies when we turned around and saw—umph!"

He staggered backward as Libby flung her arms around him, hugging him tight. He laughed and hugged her back, but not before he threw an alarmed glance his uncle's way. "What's going on?" he demanded of Uncle Frank over the top of Libby's head. "Where did that ship come from? I don't remember seeing it before! Where's the *Liberté?*"

"And why are you all dressed like that?" exclaimed Gretchen. "Did we miss some kind of switcharoo-trick out there? How did you manage to move to an entirely different *boat?*" She turned to Uncle Frank. "You even *look* different!" she continued, throwing her hands in the air, and in her consternation, she lapsed into pronouncing her w's as v's. "I svear, ve turn our backs for one second and the whole vorld changes!"

Tears leaked from Libby's eyes as she turned to her mother.

"Vhy, Libby! Vhatever is the matter? And ... have you *grown?* You look half an inch taller! Ginny, you as well! And vhy is your hair such a mess?"

Libby hugged her mom tight. "I love you so much, Mom," she said, but her voice came out in a croak. "And I—I think I understand now. I'm going to help, I promise."

As Gretchen held her daughter in her arms, her brow creased in utter befuddlement, she turned to Uncle Frank with a mildly accusatory expression. But before she could press for further details, she was distracted by the murmuring and exclamations behind them.

And she wasn't the only one. The whole party turned to see an entire marina of visitors staring at them. Some people were gesturing at the ship, some at their clothes, and everyone was chattering at once. Cell phones glinted in the sunlight: a frenzy of flashing cameras, texts and posts. Someone was recording a video. Even the man with the hamburger, whom Esmerelda had scolded to get out of the way when they'd first arrived at the marina, had completely forgotten about his mid-morning snack.

"I-I'm telling you, Eunice, I saw it change right before my eyes!" he stammered.

"I think we'd better get out of here," observed Uncle Frank. "We'll explain everything once we're back at the house."

Peter and Gretchen exchanged more worried glances, but both appeared too perplexed to argue.

"Should ve at least get the cake?" Mrs. Frye suggested shakily. "Sal, could you grab it from the boat? I know it sounds stilly but I'd hate for it to go to vaste and—vhat now?"

She let go of Libby and turned to Esmerelda, who had begun laughing so hysterically that her whole frame shook.

"C-c-cake!" the robot sputtered between guffaws.

This, of course, only made Ginny snicker … which made Libby laugh … which made Uncle Frank and Sal start to chuckle.

"Sorry, Mom," Libby managed, "but your cake won't be … um, making an appearance …."

"But-it-was-extremely-useful," offered Esmerelda, looking away, and if were possible for a robot to experience a tinge of guilt, then she definitely did.

Libby forced herself to stop laughing as she grabbed her mom's hand. Then she turned to her dad and took his. "Can we go home now?"

Ginny hooted loudly in agreement, which made Mr. and Mrs. Frye jump a little.

"Sorry," she giggled, grabbing Mrs. Frye's free hand and tugging her forward, "but that's the best idea I've heard in *centuries!*"

28

JOURNEY'S END

If you are reading this, then all has come to pass. I am finally home, as, I assume, are you. We have journeyed many roads and intersected in peculiar places. This shall be our last.

Libby held the page of her spell book closer to the candle.

"Holy Macaroni," whispered Ginny, staring at the wispy letters appearing over the back page. "How did you know to *do* that?"

You saw what I did for your Grandfather Klaus. As for the money? It was what he had left for your mother, of course; the key was in your Brothers Grimm book. You saw how I stole its secret. I felt it due me. Judge as you like.

Consider it this way: it was used for you, as it was his wealth that helped sustain me after Barvultmir was destroyed. And it was his wealth that purchased a plane ticket, a museum entrance fee ... I took only what was needed. The rest, I leave to your mother. Maybe one day she can forgive me. Maybe she can see what lengths are taken to reach the ones you love. I think she will.

I have posted the information she needs below, and I expect she will find I've been quite frugal in my thievery. As for you, child, your wealth stretches beyond bank accounts and gold. I have long known this; I believe you now know it as well.

For so many years—too many—I have watched you from afar. I have recorded your progress as best I am able, scratching away at words in my long, lonely hours. I dreamed and wished that one day your

journey would help me end mine. You see?
Wishes do come true, for I am now at peace.
And so, finally, I bid you farewell.

Always your friend (on occasion, your
enemy),

Sabine Herrmann

Ginny blew out the candle with a furious puff.

"And that," she declared, thrusting an indignant finger at the disappearing font, "is why we need a manual on The Fundamental Ethics of Witchcraft and Wizardry, ASAP!"

Libby tried very hard not to grin. "ASAP?"

"ASAP!" Ginny glowered. "I've already started a rough draft if you'd like to collaborate. I only got through Chapter One because Sal needed my help with the blimp, so I could use—"

A knock came at the bedroom door.

The door opened a crack, and a violet eye gleamed through it. A swath of long, white hair fell like a curtain before Gretchen Frye tucked it behind her ear. The door opened wider.

"You're finally up!" she exclaimed, brandishing a copy of the daily newspaper, *The Baluhla Bugle*, as if proving her point. "You girls passed out in the car and slept through an *entire day!* I don't know what happened on that ship, but whatever it was, it's turned all of you into a bunch of zombies. Even Sal and Uncle Frank conked out as soon as we all got home," she rolled up the newspaper and then placed her fists on her hips, "and Esmerelda insisted on being recharged! They've just gotten up as well! In the meantime," she continued to fuss, "what have your father and I been left with? *Nearly twenty-four hours* filled with *a lot* of unanswered questions!"

"You have no idea," Ginny giggled under her breath.

"What's that?"

"Nothing," said Libby, pressing her mouth tight in an effort to keep a straight face. "Does the paper have anything to say about our boat?"

Mrs. Frye took a deep breath and closed her eyes for a second. "I haven't read it yet—it just got delivered. And I'm not going to read it until we've had a proper celebration," she continued with an obvious attempt to contain her exasperation. "I only get to experience my daughter's eleventh birthday once, and I've already missed it!"

She marched into the room and then grabbed Libby's top hat from the bookshelf. "Now, put this on," she directed, handing the hat to Libby, "you forgot it yesterday and look what happened! Well, I'm not sure *what* happened exactly, but that's not the point! The *point* is, since *you've* apparently lost your manners and scarfed down an entire cake without me, you're just going to have to eat another one for breakfast. That's what *I've* been doing with my spare time. I—" She scowled between the two girls as they beamed back at her. "*Now* what?"

Ginny giggled. "It's just that … well, a birthday cake sounds pretty delicious right about now. It's been *ages* since I've had any of your baking!"

Gretchen made a strange huffing noise and gripped the newspaper tighter in her fist.

"We'll explain everything, Mom. I promise," Libby said, adjusting her top hat as she threw a raised eyebrow Ginny's way. "But first, we've got a surprise for you!"

Ginny nodded and mouthed the words *birthday candles* as she grabbed the spell book and skipped to the door, now beaming with so much enthusiasm that her whole head glowed bright red—even her freckles had taken on a peculiar shade of maroon. And before Mrs. Frye could protest or comment on their desperate need for a bath, the girls pulled her into the hallway.

"In-here!" called Esmerelda from the dining room. "We-are-all-waiting-for-you!"

Libby and Ginny escorted Mrs. Frye into the room, then to her seat. Esmerelda was arranging candles on the newly-baked birthday cake—practically identical to the last—while Uncle Frank and Sal were already seated at the table, each enjoying a cup of coffee, and Libby thought she'd never seen her great uncle look so delighted with a beverage in all his life.

"Look!" He declared, raising his mug as she took a seat beside him. "Real milk!"

Libby's dad glanced up from the stack of plates and forks and napkins he'd just placed on the table. "You have coffee with milk every single day, Uncle Frank." He wrinkled his nose. "But I *am* wondering about your ... er ... hygiene habits."

"Well, it feels as if it's been months, Peter, my boy!" cried Uncle Frank, oblivious to his nephew's hint. He took another sip and then winked at Libby. "Speaking of which, are we going to tackle that cake or not? I'm beginning to forget what it tastes like!"

Mr. and Mrs. Frye exchanged more glances that were starting to look more annoyed than confused, when Ginny dashed from the room, then re-appeared moments later with the kitchen fire extinguisher.

"Goodness!" cried Mrs. Frye. "I don't think we'll need *that!*"

"It's best to be prepared," said Ginny. "Just in case."

"Semper paratus!" agreed Libby, which made Sal choke on his coffee and Uncle Frank beam with pride.

And then candles were lit, Happy Birthday was sung ....

"Go on, Sassafras! What's the hold up? You suddenly too grown up for wishes?"

"Are you?" Libby peered up at her dad, doing her best to appear solemn, though in truth, she was so excited she could barely sit still. "For instance, what if you didn't have to commute so far to work anymore? Wouldn't that be a good wish? If you could start your own accounting firm?"

Peter Frye shifted in his chair. "That's ... an odd topic for your birthday! You know we can't afford to do that ...."

Libby and Ginny swapped grins, each growing wider by the second.

"But what if we *could?*" she continued, now turning to her mom. "And what if you opened your bakery in town? I've seen you check out that empty shop by the courthouse a million times—it would be perfect! What if we could do all of that? Wouldn't that be amazing?"

"Let's do this already!" said Ginny, grabbing the spell book from where it had been placed on the table. She opened it to the last page, just as Libby pushed the flickering cake in front of her mom.

"You had better speed read," advised Ginny. "This is definitely not proper fire-safety protocol."

"Read?" repeated Mrs. Frye in a fluster. "It's an empty page!"

Libby laughed, jumping up from the table and wrapping her arms around her mom's shoulders. But just as she did so, a familiar wave of nausea ripped through her head, stronger than anything she'd ever felt before. She squeezed her eyes shut, as if her eyes could block out the sickening swirl, and she suddenly felt as if she had no feet to stand on, no body to control, no voice, no sight, no ....

"Libby!" Her mother's voice barely registered in the storm of her mind. "Are you alright?"

She tried to say something, but the horror of what she was doing overwhelmed her. Not now. Not today. How could this be happening already?

She felt Uncle Frank's hand on her arm.

"Remember, Libby," he was saying quietly, so quiet she could barely hear him, or perhaps it was more as if he were speaking over a long distance—miles and miles from where she stood, "no matter what you are feeling right now, you are stronger than it."

Round and round and round. It pulsed and swirled and throbbed and sucked; growing and growing ....

But there was more than just the swirling, wasn't there? Her family. Her friends. All here, sharing together. A whole lifetime of memories, of experiences that ran far deeper than the sickening, roaring hurricane in her mind. And she thought once more of the Wizard's words, right before they stepped into the light ....

The dizzying swirls still tormented her, but she tried to think of something else, something *more*.

The storm inside of her continued, but somehow, it seemed less threatening. It was, after all, only a storm. It couldn't think. It couldn't make choices or learn or laugh or cry or love or even hate. It certainly couldn't imagine.

But she could.

She opened her eyes.

The nausea, so debilitating just moments before, slowly slipped away like a thick vapor. And she realized that her parents were right before her, fretting and hugging and smoothing hair from her sweaty forehead while just behind them, Uncle Frank sat in his mobile unit with Ginny by his side. And when she met his gaze, a spark of pride, of triumph blazed between them.

"H-holy Macaroni" exclaimed Ginny, gripping an armrest on Uncle Frank's mobile unit and accidentally pushing the spider-leg function. "Libby ... the Incident ... you-you controlled it! Right?"

"I... I think so," she answered, too shaken to know if the words actually came out, but then she felt her mother pull her into her arms.

"My brave, wonderful girl," she whispered into Libby's ear. "I don't know how or why, but I think I know what just happened. I thought such a thing would be impossible, but ... you did it. You certainly did!"

She looked into Libby's face, her beautiful, violet eyes filled with tears, but there was something else there as well. Something Libby hadn't seen in a long, long time:

Hope.

❋

It was all a bit of a blur from thereon out, but at some point, the birthday party finally resumed. All of the candles had melted into the frosting during the hubbub, so Ginny grabbed a regular taper candle and jammed it into the cake, insisting that a birthday wish required a candle .... "Not to mention a certain *font* requires it as well!" she announced a bit impatiently.

At the girls' insistence, Gretchen was once more seated in front of the cake, complete with an opened spell book practically smashed to her nose.

"Make a wish, Mom!"

"But I don't understand," she was saying in mock exasperation, but her mood had become so lightened that she couldn't keep a straight face to save her life, "why *I'm* the one supposed to make a wish! It's *your* birthday, Libby!"

"Technically, her birthday was yesterday," harrumphed Sal, who, at this point, was getting particularly grumpy over the absence of cake and a deeply anticipated TV binge. He ogled the living room couch with longing. "And anyhow, it's not like she hasn't had it before." He flicked a sour glance Libby's way. "So just make a wish for your mom, kid, and get this over with!"

Libby looked from Sal to Ginny, and then at Uncle Frank and Esmerelda. Somewhere outside the house, she heard Buttercup honking. She met her father's gaze; those hazel eyes looked quizzically back at her. Finally, she turned again to her mom.

"The problem is," she said, leaning over her mother's shoulders so that she could see the opened spell book before them, "my wish already came true."

As she spoke, the letters formed once more over the back page of the spell book. This time, Gretchen Frye's eyes locked on their forms, scanning left to right as she read, faster and faster, confusion turning to disbelief turning to … well, Libby wasn't sure what. Perhaps shock? At some point, it seemed as though her mother forgot to breathe, and when she finally finished reading, Mrs. Frye sat still as a statue, blinking mutely at the book before her until Ginny lifted it away from the candle.

Ginny clutched the book and performed a jig of sorts, not caring one iota that Uncle Frank and Sal and Mr. Frye were all staring at her as if she'd completely lost it, not to mention the decidedly judgmental glances she was getting from a robot.

"You'll understand soon enough!" she informed them.

"So make a wish, Mom," whispered Libby, and she

suddenly felt so filled with happiness that she thought she might combust. Or that she might float straight to the ceiling— no hover vent needed, no wizardly library chair required—just pure, undiluted joy.

"It's your turn now."

ABOUT THE AUTHOR

J. L. McCreedy first learned a love of writing (and developed an incurable condition of wanderlust) while growing up in Southeast Asia as the child of missionaries. She holds a B.A. in English and a law degree, freelances as a writer and consultant for charitable organizations, and whenever possible, drags her splendid husband on ill-planned adventures. She currently lives in the White Mountains of New Hampshire.

THE BALUHLA BUGLE

Tongan Ship Arrives Amid Frenzy at Biloxi Marina
BY MARDEN MAZZLETON

BILOXI—The *Mālō e Lelei*, a Tongan ship traditionally known as a Kalia, arrived yesterday, disrupting a maelstrom caused earlier by the alleged disappearance and materialization of two other ocean-going vessels. Investigations are ongoing.

Captain Kai Havea and his crew of the *Mālō e Lelei* are anchored in Biloxi for several days as part of a world-tour promoting the maritime history of the South Pacific and the Kingdom of Tonga in particular. When pressed as to why Captain Havea chose Biloxi out of hundreds of ports within the Southeast, he answered thusly:

"When I was a boy, I listened to tales my great-grandfather would tell me of his adventures on the sea. I loved them all, but my favorite story was one involving a girl. I think it was his favorite, too. Suffice it to say there is a person here whom I hope to meet, but if she reads this before we are properly acquainted, then this message is for her: I come on behalf of my late great-grandfather, of whose namesake I share. It was his dream that, one day, I might find you. He left me with a pendant he always wore—it is a bone carving of Maui's fish hook—that he wished for you to have. He said you would understand."